LATIMER BRIEFING 19

A BETTER VISION

Resources for the debate about human sexuality in the Church of England

EDITED BY MARTIN DAVIE

The Latimer Trust

ISBN 978-1-906327-45-3

Cover photo: Observation Deck binoculars© Carlos Restrepo –fotolia.com

Published by the Latimer Trust November 2016

The Latimer Trust (formerly Latimer House, Oxford) is a conservative Evangelical research organisation within the Church of England, whose main aim is to promote the history and theology of Anglicanism as understood by those in the Reformed tradition. Interested readers are welcome to consult its website for further details of its many activities.

The Latimer Trust
London N14 4PS UK
Registered Charity: 1084337
Company Number: 4104465
Web: www.latimertrust.org
E-mail: administrator@latimertrust.org

CONTENTS

Introduction

The purpose of this short booklet is to provide a brief introduction from an Evangelical perspective to the central issues involved in the debate about human sexuality that is currently taking place in the Church of England.

Parts 1 and 2 summarise two key contributions by Bishop Keith Sinclair to the 'Pilling' report of 2013, the document at the heart of the current debate. This material covers the main biblical and theological issues in the debate.

Part 3 looks at the interpretation of Scripture in the debate about human sexuality.

Part 4 explores a range of scientific issues related to the debate.

Part 5 considers how the Church can offer appropriate pastoral care to people with same sex attraction.

The material in parts 4 is and 5 is taken from resources previously posted on the website of the Evangelical Group on General Synod (EGGS) and is authored by a range of contributors (hence its varying style). It is published here with permission from EGGS.

1. The Bishop of Birkenhead's Dissenting Statement

1.1. Two points of agreement

Bishop Keith Sinclair begins his dissenting statement by agreeing with the majority report of the House of Bishops Working Group on two issues.

The first of these is the importance of 'challenging prejudice against or exclusion of those whom we perceive as being 'different' from ourselves, whatever form of difference that may take.' (Para 418). This involves not only rejecting homophobia, but also prejudice against the whole range of sexual minorities that now exist in our society.

The second is the importance of taking seriously what can be learned from the social and biological sciences about sexual attraction and thinking about how this relates to the Church's traditional teaching and reading of Scripture. In Bishop Sinclair's view the evidence we have from these sources suggests that sexual desire is 'a complex phenomenon shaped by a mysterious interplay of genetic disposition, environmental events and unconscious habits formed from previous behaviour and choices.' (Para 421). However, whatever the cause of our sexual desire the way we respond to it is something for which we are responsible and in which we are called to live in obedience to God.

1.2. The problem with the majority report

Bishop Sinclair then goes on to note that obedience to God is a key part of the Christian message.

As Bishop Sinclair sees it, the fundamental problem with the majority report is that it does not help the Church with the pastoral and missionary challenges it faces in proclaiming the call to radical discipleship and obedience in today's world and 'may even prevent the Church speaking clearly, faithfully and prophetically into the cultural debates about human sexuality.' (Para 432).

There are three reasons why this is the case.

1.3. The lack of a clear biblical vision

Firstly, the majority report lacks a clear biblical vision for sexual conduct. The teaching of the Bible, and of the Christian Church following the Bible, is that 'the sexual holiness which the resurrection life entails involves the restriction of sexual activity to the context of marriage between one man and one woman.' (Para 443). This teaching is upheld in the 1987 General Synod motion on human sexuality, but in spite of declaring that it upholds this teaching the majority report fails to provide arguments in support of it and instead undermines it 'by commending a sexual ethic based solely and simply on the values of permanence and fidelity.' (Para 448).

1.4. The issue of whether we can be sure what a proper Christian approach to sexuality should be

Secondly, not only does the report fail to argue for the Church's traditional teaching about sexuality, but it also contends that the arguments for and against this teaching should be seen as inconclusive. It is in effect saying 'we do not know what the proper Christian approach to the issue of sexuality is.' (Para 454). However, the arguments that the majority report puts forward to support this position are not, Bishop Keith says, persuasive.

On the subject of **social attitudes** the report highlights changes in attitudes to sexuality, but it fails to explore whether these changes 'are the result of the Spirit at work in the Church and society or whether they are the result of society and the Church becoming increasingly disobedient to God and deaf to what God is saying.' (Para 457). Without exploring this issue it is not possible to decide whether changes in social attitude should call us to question the Church's traditional teaching.

On the subject of **science** the report notes the continuing scientific uncertainty about the nature of same sex attraction. What it does not do, however, is look theologically at the relationship between the findings of science and the Church's traditional teaching by considering, for instance, whether the existence of same sex attraction and activity should be seen as part of God's good creation or as a result of the fall and the misuse of human autonomy. Its failure to do this theological work means that it is hard to see 'how the scientific argument can be used for not having confidence in the Church's traditional teaching.' (Para 458).

On the subject of **theology** the report emphasizes the warnings by Fr Timothy Radcliffe and Professor Oliver O'Donovan about the need to take seriously the limitations of our knowledge about sexuality and avoid closing down the debate about sexual ethics prematurely. However 'remaining open to debate is not the same thing as claiming that the Church no longer has a basis for what it has taught until now.' (Para 459). Furthermore the report does not engage with the whole range of theological evidence submitted to the Working Group and, in particular, does not engage with the new discipline of 'queer theology.' Once again the report fails to establish a theological basis for questioning the Church's traditional position.

Bishop Sinclair's overall conclusion is that the report fails to show that 'the evidence from these fields demonstrates that the theological debate about sexuality is inconclusive, or provides sufficient grounds to overturn the Church of England's previous reports and established teaching.' (Para 469). He draws attention to the fact that in the twentieth century the Church of England did not alter its traditional teaching about doctrines of the Trinity or the person of Christ just because there were those who thought that it should do so. Instead 'it continued to uphold its traditional teaching, and expected its authorized ministers to do the same, on the grounds that examination of the matter showed that the arguments against this teaching were not convincing.' (Para 471). Why, he asks, should it 'take a different approach over the issue of human sexuality than it took in relation to the debate about these doctrines'? (Para 471).

1.5. The proposal for liturgies to mark same-sex relationships

Thirdly, the majority report suggests that with the permission of the relevant PCC a priest should be free to mark liturgically in a public service the formation of a permanent same sex relationship. Bishop Sinclair argues that if adopted this suggestion would lead to:

....the cultural captivity of the Church, inhibiting her ability to proclaim the biblical and Christian teaching about sexual ethics and the power of Jesus Christ to liberate people from sin, including sexual sin. The Church will lack credibility in declaring that sexual activity is given exclusively for heterosexual marriage, or in declaring that people can and should refrain from same-sex sexual activity, once it is holding authorized services that affirm sexually active gay and lesbian relationships. Pressure is also likely to grow for liturgical recognition of non-marital sexual relationships. (Para 480).

Furthermore, he says, we need to be clear that 'even if what is proposed are not called blessings, that is in fact what they will be. They will be occasions when God's blessing is invoked on a same sex relationship.' (Para 481). He then quotes the words of the Canadian theologian Edith Humphrey who says that invoking God's blessing in this way 'would be to name God as the one who blesses an act for which repentance is required. So we would replace God with an idol, and so would rend the Church.' (Para 481).

1.6. *The hallmarks of a better vision*

Because the majority report is flawed in the ways highlighted above, Bishop Sinclair does not think it provides a suitable basis for the proposed facilitated conversations on human sexuality. He also thinks that if the report or its recommendations/endorsements was accepted by the Church of England the resulting perception that the Church of England had decided to walk away from traditional Christian teaching on sexuality would be damaging to relationships within the Church of England and the Anglican Communion and with other churches as well.

As an alternative to the approach taken by the majority report, Bishop Sinclair finishes his dissenting statement by setting out eight hallmarks of a 'better vision.'

a. It affirms God's love and concern for all, whatever their sexuality, recognising we are all sinners whose only hope is in the love of God shown to us in Jesus Christ and poured into our hearts by the Holy Spirit.

b. It seeks to be marked by love, truth and grace in ongoing debates, repudiating and regretting all attitudes and actions which victimise or diminish people whose sexual attraction is directed towards people of the same sex or towards people of both sexes

c. It commends marriage as an institution lovingly created by God in which one man and one woman enter into an exclusive relationship for life, believing this to be the only form of partnership approved by God for sexual relations and thus the only form of sexual partnership that properly expresses love for God.

d. It encourages churches to be safe spaces where everyone, including those with same-sex attraction or bisexual attraction, is able to share and explore his or her story with fellow believers for mutual encouragement and support as we help each other grow together into maturity in Christ.

e. It commends and encourages all who experience same-sex or bisexual attraction and have committed themselves to chastity by refraining from homoerotic sexual practice, welcoming as leaders those of them God calls to ordination.

f. It supports all those who responsibly seek to help Christians who experience sexual attractions in conflict with their commitment to live in accordance with biblical teaching, encouraging the Church to offer all Christians counsel and pastoral support to live a chaste life.

g. It calls on churches to welcome and accept all, whatever their sexuality and whether or not they follow the Church's teaching on sexual behaviour, in the hope that, like all of us who are living outside God's purposes, they will come in due course to see the need to be transformed and live lives of loving obedience in accordance with biblical revelation and orthodox Church teaching.

h. It calls on churches not to be conformed to the prevailing sexual culture, but to seek to resist and transform it so that both the Church and wider society will flourish by more closely reflecting God's standards in their beliefs about sexuality and their sexual behaviour. (Para 488).

2. Scripture and same sex relationships

'Scripture and same sex relationships' is a paper which Bishop Keith Sinclair submitted to the House of Bishops Working Group on Human Sexuality and which was subsequently published as Appendix 3 of the Working Group's report. The page references below are to those in the report.

As Bishop Sinclair explains in his introduction, the argument of his paper is that 'the God who reveals to us the nature of love in his creation of the world, in his calling of Israel, in his incarnation and atoning death, in his resurrection and promise of a new heaven and a new earth' has 'set limits and boundaries to the sexual expressions of 'love' for those who are attracted to those of their own gender' and that he has done this because of his love. (p 158).

This, he says, has always been the teaching of the Church and the findings of biblical scholarship have not shown that the reading of the Bible that underlies this teaching is mistaken.

2.1. *Three contexts that need to be borne in mind*

Bishop Sinclair then goes on to look at three contexts which need to be borne in mind when considering the teaching of Scripture about same sex relationships.

The first context is the overall biblical story stretching from Genesis to Revelation about the coming together of heaven and earth, the two halves of God's good creation. In the Bible, in passages such as Ephesians 5 and Revelation 21, the union of husband and wife in marriage symbolizes this coming together of heaven and earth achieved through the work of Christ.

The second context is the first century Jewish context in which Jews accepted the Levitical prohibition of same sex relationships on the grounds that these were not part of God's good creation and were opposed to pagan forms of behaviour that contravened this prohibition and God's created order.

The third context is the first century pagan context in which there was a wide range of same sex sexual activity (including quasi-marital unions) and a polarization between those who accepted such activity and those who were appalled by it. In the light of this pagan context it is difficult to assert that 'first-century Christians did not know about the kind of homosexual practice that is being commended today.' (p 162).

2.2.   *The teaching and practice of Jesus*

He next looks at the teaching and practice of Jesus and argues that what we find in passages such as Matthew 19:1-12 is that 'Jesus' kingdom agenda envisages, not the abandonment or reframing of male-female marriage, but its firming up and re-establishment.' (p 164). What we find in the gospels is that:

> Jesus challenges us to a righteousness that exceeds that of the Scribes and Pharisees and calls us to a love that includes all that will come, be cleansed, healed and forgiven in the kingdom of God. Jesus was not afraid to challenge misunderstandings of God's will – ''You have heard it said ... but I say to you ...' – but nowhere do we have a record of doing so on same sex unions and his general teaching in sexual matters is more rigorist (e.g. adultery in the heart) not more lax. (p 164).

2.3.   *The teaching of Paul*

Moving on to the teaching of Paul, Bishop Sinclair notes that in passages such as Colossians 3:1-11 and Ephesians 4:17–5:20 Paul assumes 'that his congregations would stand out from the surrounding pagan world, not least by their refusal to behave in the way that pagans did, not least in regard to sex.' (p 165). It is impossible, he says 'to read either passage, knowing the Jewish and pagan worlds of the day, and then to conclude (as people regularly try to do) that Paul would have made an exception had he known about 'permanent, faithful, stable' same-sex relationships.' (p 165). Paul was 'a theologian of creation renewed' and this meant he rejected forms of behaviour, such as same sex relationships, that were incompatible with creation.

Bishop Sinclair's overall conclusion is that the New Testament texts that refer to same sex relationships are not odd and isolated texts that stand outside the mainstream of biblical thought. They are instead texts that are expressive of the fundamental Jewish world view that was re-affirmed by the early Christians on the basis of the teaching of Jesus himself. As Bishop Keith puts it:

The texts in question are visibly and demonstrably symptomatic of the larger Jewish worldview at a point where it was strongly and emphatically re-affirmed by the early Christians, drawing on Jesus' warnings about the evils which come from the heart and about the transformation and healing which was necessary and was offered (not least through his cross and resurrection). (p 172).

2.4. Bishop Tom Wright on adiaphora

At the end of his paper Bishop Keith includes an executive summary of a paper given by Bishop Tom Wright to the Durham Diocesan Synod in May 2010. In this paper Bishop Wright argues that it cannot be simply assumed a matter should be seen as *adiaphora*, something on which Christians may agree to live with different approaches. Rather, this is something that needs to be decided as the result of a debate about the matter at the appropriate level in the life of the Church. He further notes that the Anglican approach has been to decide whether a proposed innovation can be accepted as *adiaphora* by first discussing the matter at the Lambeth Conference and then, if agreed there, the matter goes to the provinces of the communion and then to the dioceses and parishes.[1]

---

[1]   Since Bishop Keith wrote his paper Tom Wright has also contributed an important chapter on 'Pastoral Theology for Perplexing Topics: Paul and *Adiaphora*' to Andrew Atherstone and Andrew Goddard (eds), *Good Disagreement? Grace and Truth in a Divided Church*, Oxford: Lion 2015.

3. The interpretation of Scripture in the current debate

3.1. *The key questions regarding the interpretation of Scripture.*

A central part of the debate about human sexuality has been a debate about the interpretation of Scripture in relation to this issue between revisionist scholars such as James Brownson, Tobias Haller and Theodore Jennings on the one hand and traditionalist scholars such as Michael Brown, Robert Gagnon and Ian Paul on the other.

The key questions raised in the debate between these scholars are as follows:

a. Should we see all Scripture as equally authoritative, or can we affirm some parts of it and not others, and if so, on what basis?

b. Do the creation narratives in Genesis 1 and 2 give us a normative account of human sexuality and the nature of marriage?

c. What, if anything, can we learn from the stories about Sodom and Gibeah in Genesis 19 and Judges 19 that is relevant to the contemporary debate about same-sex relationships?

d. What exactly is prohibited in Leviticus 18:22 and 20:13 and is this prohibition still binding under the new covenant?

e. Does what is said about sacred prostitution in Deuteronomy 23:17-18 have anything to contribute to the debate about same-sex relationships?

f. What is the point that St. Paul is making in Romans 1:26-27 when he describes sexual activity between women and women and men and men as 'contrary to nature' (*para phusin*)? Does he regard such activity as sinful and is the real point of this passage in Romans not to condemn particular forms of sin, but to rebuke the self-righteousness that thinks it is right to judge others?

g. Do the terms used by St. Paul in 1 Corinthians 6:9-11 and 1 Timothy 1:10 (*arsenokoitai* and *malakoi*) refer to same-sex sexual activity and, if they do, are they referring to pederasty and sexual exploitation?

h. Does Jude 7 teach that Sodom and the surrounding cities were condemned for homosexual lust or the desire for sex with angels?

i.   What do the teaching and practice of Jesus recorded in the gospels contribute to our thinking about same-sex relationships?

j.   Are there examples of same-sex relationships which are viewed positively in the Bible, such as, for example, the relationships between Ruth and Naomi, David and Jonathan and Jesus and the beloved disciple?

3.2.   How should we respond to these questions?

3.2.1.   Should we see all Scripture as equally authoritative, or can we affirm some parts of it and not others, and if so, on what basis?

Because all Scripture is God's word (Psalm 119:105, Ephesians 6:17) inspired by God's Spirit (2 Timothy 3:16, 2 Peter 1:21) it is not legitimate to affirm some parts of it and not others, or a legitimate form of hermeneutics to interpret some parts of it in a way that conflicts with other parts of it.

As Bishop Sinclair suggests, Scripture needs to be read as a God given unity with a single overall coherent message. Part of reading it in this way involves understanding that although parts of the Old Testament law are no longer binding on Christians because they have been fulfilled and transcended through the work of Christ, the basic moral law of the Old Testament, including its teaching on sexuality still applies today.

3.2.2.   Do the creation narratives in Genesis 1 and 2 give us a normative account of human sexuality and the nature of marriage?

Within the biblical canon the creation narratives in Genesis 1-2 lay down the basic parameters for what it means to live rightly as human beings created by God. They teach that God created human beings as male and female to be his image bearers, ruling over creation on his behalf and being fruitful and multiplying (Genesis 1:26-28). Marriage, which corresponds to this vocation, was ordained by God as a life-long, exclusive relationship between one man and one woman (Genesis 2:24) in which sexual activity unites spouses to one another in love and leads to the birth of children.

3.2.3. What, if anything, can we learn from the stories about Sodom and Gibeah in Genesis 19 and Judges 19 that is relevant to the contemporary debate about same-sex relationships?

When understood in their canonical context the stories of Sodom and Gibeah in Genesis 19 and Judges 19 indicate that the desire for homosexual sex is a symptom of the wider sinfulness of a society that has turned away from God. Although this is often suggested, there is nothing in Genesis 19 to suggest that it is concerned with gang rape. Hebrew has a vocabulary to describe rape and it is not used in this text. All that Genesis 19:5 tells us is that the men of Sodom wanted to have sex with lot's visitors. It does not limit what the men of Sodom was contemplating to rape even if the context suggests that this may have been what the crowd had in mind.

3.2.4. What exactly is prohibited in Leviticus 18:22 and 20:13 and is this prohibition still binding under the new covenant?

What Leviticus 18:22 and 20:13 prohibit without qualification is sex between men. There is no reference to specific forms of sex such as anal penetration and no restriction of the prohibition to Israelites or the land of Israel.

An analysis of the structure Leviticus 20 indicates that sex between men was prohibited, like a range of other forms of sexual activity, because it came under the overall category of 'adultery.' That is to say, the starting point for thinking about sexuality in the Law of Moses is a marriage between one man and one woman in line with the way that God created the human race. All the prohibited sexual offences are offences because in various ways they involve sex outside this context, sex before marriage, with someone other than your wife, sex with someone of the same sex, or sex with another species. The issue is therefore the way that God has created the world and the calling of human beings to behave in a way that corresponds to that.

Lesbianism would also seem to fit into this list of prohibitions and, as the Rabbis thought, a prohibition of lesbianism may be implicit in the general prohibition in Leviticus 18:3 against following the practices of the Egyptians and the Canaanites, or prohibitions in the masculine singular may have been seen as applying generically to both men and women. Certainly Romans 1:26-27 shows that St. Paul understood the prohibitions as applying inclusively to both sexes.

3.2.5. Does what is said about sacred prostitution in Deuteronomy 23:17-18 have anything to contribute to the debate about same-sex relationships?

Deuteronomy 23:17-18 reinforces the Old Testament witness against all forms of homosexual activity by referring to male homosexual prostitution as 'abomination' even though homosexual prostitution in the context of cultic activity was the most culturally acceptable form of same-sex sexual activity in the Ancient Near Eastern context.

3.2.6. What is the point that St. Paul is making in Romans 1:26-27 when he describes sexual activity between women and women and men and men as 'contrary to nature' (para phusin)? Does he regard such activity as sinful and is the real point of this passage in Romans not to condemn particular forms of sin, but to rebuke the self-righteousness that thinks it is right to judge others?

It is true (as a number of scholars have pointed out) that the term 'contrary to nature' used in Romans 1:26-27 does not necessarily mean 'sinful.' However, given that the context of Romans 1:18-32 is all about sinful behaviour, given the other terms used in these verses 'dishonourable passions,' shameless acts' and 'the due penalty for their error' and given that 'contrary to nature' was a term regularly used by both Gentile and Jewish writers to explain why homosexual acts were wrong, the term clearly does mean sinful in this instance. What Paul is saying is that both gay and lesbian behaviour is wrong because it goes against the pattern for sexual behaviour established by God at creation and is in that sense 'contrary to nature.'

It is also true that St. Paul's big point in Romans 1:16-3:31 is indeed to attack self-righteousness and replace it with an acceptance that everyone alike is sinful and that everyone alike can only be saved through the action of God in Christ received by faith, this argument actually demands that the behaviour described in Genesis 1:18-32 (including the behaviour described in Romans 1:26-27) truly is sinful. Paul's rhetorical strategy is to establish that Gentiles are sinners in Romans 1, that Jews are sinners in Romans 2 and that all alike are sinners in Romans 3 thus leading to the conclusion that all alike need salvation through faith in Christ.

The structure of St. Paul's argument thus demands that he sees the homosexual conduct described in Romans 1:26-27 as really sinful and one of the reasons that the saving work of Christ is required. It is one of the ways in which 'all have sinned and fall short of the glory of God' (Romans 3:23).

3.2.7. Do the terms used by St. Paul in 1 Corinthians 6:9-11 and 1 Timothy 1:10 (arsenokoitai and malakoi) refer to same-sex sexual activity and, if they do, are they referring to pederasty and sexual exploitation?

The evidence points to St. Paul using *arsenokoitai* and *malakoi* in I Corinthians 6:9-11 to describe the active and passive partners in male homosexual intercourse and to his using *arsenokoitai* on its own in I Timothy 1:10 to refer to male homosexual activity in general. It also points to *arsenokoitai* being based on the word used in the Greek translation of the Old Testament, the Septuagint, to describe male same-sex activity in Leviticus 18:22 and 20:13.

There is nothing in the terms themselves or the context in which they are used to suggest that St. Paul is using them to refer to pederastic or exploitative same-sex activity. What he is making clear in both passages is that the Levitical prohibitions against same-sex relationships are still in force (and refer to Gentiles as well as Jews) and that such relationships are to be repudiated by Christians as contrary to the new status they have in Christ (I Corinthians) and as contrary to the 'gospel' and 'sound doctrine' (I Timothy).

3.2.8. Does Jude 7 teach that Sodom and the surrounding cities were condemned for homosexual lust or the desire for sex with angels?

The story in Genesis 19 itself, the subsequent Jewish interpretation of that story which forms the background to Jude 7 and the way what Jude says is interpreted in 2 Peter 2:7 and 10 all tell against the idea that the 'going after other flesh' in Jude 7 means seeking to have sex with angels. The most likely readings are that the phrase should be interpreted as 'desiring homosexual sex' or that it means 'by [or in the course of] committing sexual immorality they lusted after other flesh' by inadvertently seeking to have sex with angels. In both cases homosexual desire is seen as reason for God's judgment.

Like Ezekiel 16:49-50, Jude 7 and 2 Peter 2:6-10 are biblical passages referring to the Sodom story which indicate that it is to be seen as story about God's judgement on the desire for homosexual sex.

3.2.9. *What do the teaching and practice of Jesus recorded in the gospels contribute to our thinking about same-sex relationships?*

The fact that there are no controversies about homosexuality in the gospels indicates that Jesus accepted the Jewish belief that same-sex activity was forbidden by the Mosaic Law. If Jesus had supported same-sex relationships, then this would have caused enormous controversy and there would be a record of this in the Gospels, just as there is a record of the ways in which he challenged the thinking of his contemporaries on other matters.

However, as Bishop Sinclair notes, we are not left simply with the argument from silence. The record of Jesus' teaching in the gospels points us in the same direction. It tells us:

- That Jesus founded his sexual ethic on the fact that God created human beings as male and female and joined them together in marriage as recorded in Genesis 1 and 2 (Matthew 19:1-9, Mark 10:2-12).

- That Jesus did not reject the teaching of the Mosaic Law on sexual ethics, but rather intensified it by including desire as well as action and by taking a stricter line on divorce (Matthew 5:27-32).

- That Jesus included *porneia* as one of those things that renders an individual unclean in the sight of God (Matthew 5:19, Mark 7:21). The lexical evidence suggests that *porneia* was a catch all term that included not only adultery, but also incest, homosexuality and bestiality. Obviously, Jesus himself probably did not use the actual term *porneia* because he would normally have spoken in Aramaic rather than Greek, but by using this term Matthew and Mark are testifying that Jesus regarded homosexuality as something that made people unclean before God.

The appeal made by some revisionist writers to Jesus' saying about eunuchs (Mathew 19:10-12) or the story of his healing of the centurion's servant (Matthew 8:5-13, Luke 7:1-10) as indicating that Jesus approved of same-sex relationships is a misinterpretation of these passages. What Jesus says about eunuchs tells us that he saw the only alternative to (heterosexual) marriage as celibacy and in the case of the story of the centurion's servant: (a) there is nothing in the language used in the story to indicate a sexual relationship, (b) the Jewish authorities would not have regarded the centurion as a 'righteous man' had he been in such a relationship, (c) Jesus endorsement of such a relationship would have meant endorsement of a exploitative relationship involving pederasty and probably rape.

3.2.10. *Are there examples of same-sex relationships which are viewed positively in the Bible, such as, for example, the relationships between Ruth and Naomi, David and Jonathan and Jesus and the beloved disciple?*

There is no evidence to support the idea that Ruth and Naomi, David and Jonathan or Jesus and the beloved disciple are examples of lesbian or gay relationships. What they do point to, however, is the importance of strong loving friendships between people of the same sex.

The fact that neither in the case of these examples, nor anywhere else in Scripture, are there any positive depictions of same-sex sexual relationships, let alone same-sex 'marriages', highlights the point made by the American writer Michael Brown that 'the Bible is a heterosexual book' in the sense that 'From Genesis to Revelation the Bible presents and presupposes heterosexuality as the divinely intended norm'.[1] Everything that the Bible says about sex and marriage reflects God's original creation of human beings as male and female and marriage between men and women as the context in which sexual activity finds its proper place.

3.3.   *For further reading*

Revisionist writers

James Brownson, *Bible, Gender, Sexuality*, Grand Rapids/Cambridge: Eerdmans, 2013.

Tobias Haller, *Reasonable and Holy*, New York: Seabury Books, 2009.

Theodore Jennings, *The Man Jesus Loved: Homoerotic Narratives from the New Testament*, Cleveland: Pilgrim Press, 2003.

Theodore Jennings, *Jacob's Wound – homoerotic narrative in the literature of Ancient Israel*, New York & London, Continuum, 2005.

Matthew Vines, *God and the Gay Christian*, New York, Convergent Books, 2014.

Traditionalist writers

Michael Brown, *Can you be Gay and Christian?* Lake Mary: Front line, 2014.

Richard Davidson, *Flame of Yahweh*, Peabody: Hendrickson, 2007.

Martin Davie, *Studies on the Bible and same-sex relationships since 2003*, Gilead Books 2014.

Robert Gagnon, *The Bible and Homosexual Practice*, Abingdon Press, 2001.

Ian Paul, *Same Sex Unions – The Key Biblical Texts*, Grove Books, 2014.

---

[1]   Michael L Brown, *Can you be Gay and Christian?* p 83.

4. Science and the current debate

4.1. Science and Human Sexuality

When we talk about the morality of different kinds of sexual interests, the question of 'what science tells us' often comes into the conversation. The point usually being made is that we now know much more about human sexuality than in biblical times so we need to revise or update our thinking about the moral issues as well.

The question of how science relates to our understanding of human sexuality in fact has a long and controversial history. On one side of the debate, people have sometimes used labels of illness to pathologise and humiliate people considered to be different from them. Until 1973, for example, homosexuality was considered by psychiatrists to be an illness in need of a cure. On the other side, revisionist theologians have sometimes deployed science (without really understanding it) to imply that the Bible no longer has anything relevant to say on this issue. So we need to think carefully about how science works, and what it can actually contribute to serious theological debate and moral reasoning in this area. And we need to be especially vigilant to the way that science is used (on all sides) for political leverage and point scoring.

It is not possible here to review the vast number of (often contradictory) scientific claims about the complex area of human sexual interests. But we do need to consider the more fundamental questions that lie behind them.

4.2. The latest scientific discoveries often turn out to be wrong

Science is the pursuit of knowledge and understanding of the natural and social world based on painstaking observational evidence and repeated experimentation. The conclusions of scientific thinking are most reliable when they have been tested repeatedly under experimental (controlled) conditions. But in many areas it is difficult to carry out repeat tests under laboratory-type conditions. The vagaries of the 'science' of economics is a case in point. And in complex areas such as the study of human behaviour, individual observations have to be merged to create bigger theories, or stories, to try to explain what is going on, and these are extremely difficult to test experimentally under controlled conditions. That is why we get newspaper headlines of 'study proves X' one day, and then 'study disproves X' the next, each backed up with pie charts and professorial talking heads.

Science methodology has delivered enormous social and material goods for human civilisation. But when we hear about the latest science claims in the sphere of sexuality, we should retain a healthy scepticism: there is no substitute for checking the facts carefully for ourselves and asking: Are these claims really justified by the evidence? The popular notion that there is a 'gay gene' is a good example of how small unproven studies may be seized on, popularised and then used by media elites to shape a whole new cultural understanding of the way things work. But as we see in another article, the evidence for a 'gay gene' turned out to be very weak indeed.

4.3.   Science and morality function in different categories

Even when a scientific discovery seems reasonably reliable, we need to be careful about using it to support a particular line of moral reasoning. Science can help us to map and investigate our experiences, but it can't interpret them or answer questions about moral value. Science can help us to understand factors that predispose us to experiencing certain attractions, and it can make predictions about the outcomes of different courses of action, but it can't tell us what we should actually do about our wants and desires. These are different categories of analysis and we shouldn't confuse them.

Take the case of promiscuity. Certain genetic profiles may turn out to be linked with a tendency toward seeking 'one-night stands', especially those genes, or groups of genes, that are associated with personality traits such as impulsiveness and novelty-seeking. But that doesn't absolve us from the need to test our desires against moral standards and beliefs and to control our behaviour in line with them. So when we hear the latest claims about science and 'what we now know', we should handle with care: science can't settle the moral status of different human sexual interests.

4.4.   Are people born gay?

The notion that people are 'born gay' provides a good example of how preliminary scientific findings can be seized upon, politicised and then embedded in culture as an indisputable fact that 'everybody knows' is true.

Twenty years ago a study claimed to have found a specific gene linked to male sexual orientation. The study was never replicated but it helped to spawn the idea that there are just two groups of people – gay or straight – whose sexual interests and attractions are somehow fixed at birth.

Since then the evidence for a genetic cause has weakened considerably. Genes contribute to the development of our sexual desires and interests – just as they contribute to the development of personality traits such as humility and compassion. But whatever our attractions and instinctive interests, they are almost certainly the result of a complex interplay between genes and environment. And of course all kinds of factors come into play as we decide whether and how to act upon our attractions and desires.

The 'born gay' theory also implies that our sexual interests are fixed and inflexible. But the more reliable surveys (all of them have problems of accuracy) now suggest that bisexuality is the most common identity label chosen by women. And there is a growing body of evidence to suggest that for many men, too, sexuality can be experienced as more fluid and changeable.

This complexity does not diminish the reality that a minority of men and women experience same-sex attraction as a powerful experience throughout their lives. But we need to recognise that it is but one part of a larger, more flexible, picture of human sexuality and we should certainly think carefully before saddling children and young people with identity-fixing labels. Many faithful Christians, whether or not they believe they were born gay, prefer their given identity in Christ as the basis on which to order and discipline their sexual interests and desires.

4.5.   Can Sexuality Change?

4.5.1.   Does sexuality change naturally?

Some people do experience a shift in sexual attractions from homosexual to heterosexual or vice versa. In a recent paper for the Archive of Sexual Behaviour, Michael King (who is the chair of the Royal College of Psychiatrists' Gay and Lesbian Special Interest Group and openly homosexual) and others looked at the correlation between how men and women described their sexual orientation, and alongside that gave a report of their sexual partnership status. Of the almost 3,500 participants who described themselves as 'entirely heterosexual' or 'mostly heterosexual', 23 said that their choice for sexual partner was 'mainly same sex' or 'only same sex'. This constituted 0.6% of the population. However, when the same question was asked of the 44 participants who described themselves as 'mostly homosexual' or 'entirely homosexual', 8 said that their choice of sexual partner was 'only opposite sex' or 'more often opposite sex'. This constituted almost 20% of the group, or proportionally 30 times as many as those who were heterosexual but mainly had homosexual relationships.

This suggests that sexual identity, sexual orientation and sexual practice are not necessarily one and the same.

In another significant study, the 2003 piece by Dickson, Paul and Herbison, as part of a cohort study of women born 1972/1973, the researchers explored sexual behaviour over time. Of the eight women who at age 21 claimed a major attraction to those of the same sex, five years later two of them (25%) now claimed to be exclusively opposite-sex attracted, and a further three (37.5%) claimed only to have occasional same-sex attractions. Meanwhile, three of the 390 women (< 1%) who reported exclusive heterosexual attraction at age 21 reported major homosexual attraction at age 26, and a further 42 (just over 10%) reported some homosexual attraction.

A ten-year US longitudinal study by Mock and Eibach also built up a picture of a bipolar sexual orientation spectrum with transition both ways. Transition was far more likely from homosexual/bisexual towards another orientation than from heterosexuality towards bisexuality/homosexuality. This effect is more pronounced amongst women than men.

More recent research by Lisa Diamond indicates that even amongst men and women who identify as exclusively homosexual, there are large proportions who also report sexual encounters with those of the opposite sex.

4.5.2. Can sexuality change through therapy?

The main longitudinal study of so-called 'reparative therapy' was carried out by Stanton Jones and Mark Yarhouse. This research used psychotherapy industry standard measures to assess whether sexual orientation of participants changed, and whether the therapy caused psychological harm to the participants.

On average, Jones and Yarhouse observed a small recordable orientation shift in those who participated, but not a significant one. However, for those who began the therapy self-reporting as almost exclusively homosexual in their attractions, there was a more noticeable shift in orientation that was significant. This seemed to indicate that therapy was more likely to be successful at helping those who had exclusive homosexuality to develop some heterosexual feelings, but it didn't provide anything like a 'gay to straight' outcome.

At the time, sexual orientation was usually measured on a single bipolar scale between exclusively homosexual and exclusively heterosexual (the so-called Kinsey Scale). But when participants were asked to measure homosexual attraction and heterosexual attraction on separate scales (i.e. not in relation to each other) then the change was more substantial. For the whole population there was a significant reduction in homosexual attraction. The more pronounced a participant's homosexual orientation was to begin with, the more pronounced the reduction in their homosexual attraction. However, there was no significant increase in heterosexual attraction, though on average participants did record some increase.

Jones and Yarhouse also asked participants to report what they felt were the results of the therapy. Over two-thirds of the participants reported a positive desired change with respect to their sexuality. NB this included now being able to live a chaste life, or feeling positive about continuing in therapy. One in eight of the participants reported that they had rejected the premise of the therapy and were definitely gay, or that they were confused about their sexual identity. Significantly, not only was there no clinical evidence that reparative therapy caused harm, there was a significant decrease in the distress reported by participants.

So, studies of homosexuals who haven't sought to change their orientation show that for some people sexuality changes naturally over the years. Specifically, female homosexuality seems to be more fluid than male. This fits with the twin studies which suggest a potentially higher environmental factor for homosexuality amongst women than men.

Where people have tried to change through therapy the evidence is that some experience change when they participate. Whilst some have not experienced much or any change in their sexual feelings, there has been real change for a minority, whether in terms of a reduction in the strength of their same-sex attractions, an increase in their opposite-sex attraction, or both. Certainly, the best longitudinal study so far found no evidence that such therapy is psychologically damaging, even where it does not achieve the results the participant wanted, and it can have other benefits such as reducing the person's distress. So, whilst therapeutic approaches which seek to change sexual orientation have no guarantee of success, there is no reason for people not to have such therapy where they wish to do so. Of course, people need to be informed and realistic about the potential outcomes, as they should be when entering any therapy, and the therapy must be responsible and professional.

4.6.   For further reading

Glynn Harrison, 'Sexuality and the politicisation of science' http://glynnharrison.wordpress.com/2014/07/09/sexuality-and-the-politicisation-of-science/

Stanton L. Jones, 'Same Sex Science' http://www.firstthings.com/article/2012/02/same-sex-science

P. Ould, 'Can your sexuality change?' http://www.livingout.org/can-your-sexuality-change-

D. De Pomeroi 'The Witness of Science' in P. Groves, *The Anglican Communion and Homosexuality*, SPCK, 2010.

Jeffrey Satinover, *Homosexuality and the Politics of Truth*, Grand Rapids: Baker Books, 1996.

Mark A. Yarhouse and Stanton L. Jones, 'Honest Sex-Science' http://www.firstthings.com/article/2012/10/honest-sex-science

5. Issues about pastoral care

5.1. *How can we ensure that LGBT+ people feel welcome in our churches?*

On the whole, the answer to this question is deceptively simple: the way we welcome LGBT+ people is the same way we should welcome everyone! We greet them warmly, we get to know them, we show them hospitality. It is important not to think that because of their sexuality, the situation of LGBT+ people is different or more problematic than anyone else's. They need and have the right to be treated with love and dignity.

So, LGBT+ people don't need to be welcomed differently because of their sexuality. But because of the way that at least some, perhaps many, LGBT+ people have been treated by the Church, there are some positive things which Church members and leaders can do. But these need to be done because of the situation of LGBT+ people with respect to the Church, not because they are LGBT+ as such.

Ask them how much they are willing to share their story and journey with you, and listen to what they are willing to share. This is always a privilege! If they have been hurt by the Church in the past, acknowledge this and take it seriously.

Ask them what they would find helpful. A gay couple wanted to do an evangelistic course at a church, and the pastor invited them for dinner beforehand. Without setting aside what he believed, he explained he wanted them to feel completely welcome and he asked if there was anything he could do to ensure that. He asked them to let him know if they encountered any homophobia on the course. In doing so, he acknowledged not only that they needed to feel welcomed, but that they already had something to offer and teach the church.

Be consistent. If you let unmarried opposite-sex couples share a room at the church weekend away, you should do the same with a gay couple. If you baptise members of or the children of cohabiting opposite-sex couples, baptise members of or the children of same-sex couples. And don't hold LGBT+ people to different standards when it comes to responsibility and leadership.

The pastoral advice on how to make their situation right before God will, of course, be different for gay couples and for opposite-sex unmarried couples, since marriage is a solution for opposite-sex couples, but not for those of the same sex, who will need to cease any form of sexual relationship. This difference is very important, but it should not affect overall consistency of treatment on other matters.

How do we welcome everyone without NECESSARILY endorsing their beliefs or choices?

The church is called to welcome everyone, just as God welcomes every one of us 'while we were still sinners' (Romans 5:8).

It is essential to welcome same-sex couples and single gay people who are not already signed up to the biblical teaching about sex in exactly the same way we would welcome anyone else. Most church leaders minister frequently amongst couples who are cohabiting and, especially if one or more of the couple are Christians, there will come a point for a gentle but honest conversation about how this relates to their following of Christ. But it is not the first or the dominant topic of conversation! The first priority is to ensure that they are welcomed, and treated with love and respect. This is what they need first and foremost, in order that as they meet with God, receive good teaching and grow in maturity, they will surrender their lives more fully to him.

Jesus obviously held his moral convictions consistently, yet he did not hesitate to respond differently to different individuals according to what they needed (needed, not in the sense of what they thought they needed, of course, but in the sense of what he could see they truly needed). One response for the rich young ruler (dramatic challenge to sell everything), another for the woman caught in adultery (saving her life and pronouncing forgiveness before enjoining her not to sin any longer), yet another towards the men who brought the woman to him (exposing their own adultery). Holding our convictions without compromise doesn't automatically imply pronouncing them at every opportunity.

So, if a gay person or same-sex couple are part of a church or start attending a church, their immediate need is almost certainly not to be confronted personally with the biblical teaching about sex (although it is something that church leaders should regularly teach on publicly). Because of media coverage, they will almost certainly be perfectly well aware of what most Christians believe and churches teach about sex! What they will primarily need is to be welcomed warmly, loved and accepted just as they are, and offered a safe environment in which to grow in their faith – not because we don't want them to live according to biblical teaching, but precisely because we want this for them.

5.2. How can churches help Christians with same-sex attraction?

The place where all Christians should receive encouragement and support as they seek to follow Christ is in their local church. Same-sex attraction is no more inherently problematic than any other temptation that Christians face, but here are a number of things that churches can particularly do to help Christians with same-sex attraction:

5.2.1. Make it easy to talk about

Both pastors and church members need to know that there will likely be some within their own church family for whom same-sex attraction is a painful and personal struggle. When the issue comes up in the life of the church, it needs to be recognized that this is an issue Christians wrestle with too, and that the church needs to be ready and equipped to walk alongside such brothers and sisters.

Many Christians still speak of homosexuality in hurtful and pejorative ways. Christians who should know better still use phrases like, "that's so gay" to describe something they don't like. Such comments are only going to make their same-sex attracted Christian brothers and sisters feel unable to open up. When I first began to share of my own experiences of same-sex attraction with friends at church, I was struck by how many (even mature) Christians felt they needed to apologize for comments they'd made in the past about homosexuality that they now realized may have been hurtful.

Having made it easy for someone to talk about their same-sex attraction, we must not then make the mistake of always talking to them about it! They may want us to ask about how things are going from time to time, but to make this the main or only thing you talk about with them can be problematic: it may reinforce the false idea that this is who they really are, and it may actually overlook other issues that they may need to talk about more than same-sex attraction. Sexuality may not be their greatest battle.

5.2.2. Honour singleness

Those for whom marriage is not a realistic prospect need to be affirmed in their calling to singleness. The church needs to uphold and honour singleness as a gift and take care not to unwittingly denigrate it. Singles should not be thought of – still less spoken of – as loose ends that need tying up. And pastors should not assume every single person is so because they've been too lazy to look for a marriage partner.

5.2.3. Remember that church is family

Paul repeatedly refers to the local church as the "household of God" (for example, 1 Timothy 3:15). It is the family of God, and Christians are to be family to one another. Paul encourages Timothy to treat older men as fathers, "younger men as brothers, older women as mothers, younger women as sisters" (1 Timothy 5:1-2). The church is to think of itself as immediate family. Nuclear families within the church need the input and involvement of the wider church family; they are not designed to be self-contained. Those that open up their family life to others find that it is a great two-way blessing. Single people get to experience some of the joys of family life, children get to benefit from the influence of other older Christians, parents get to have the encouragement of others supporting them, and families as a whole get to learn something of what it means to serve and be outward-looking as a family.

5.2.4. Deal with biblical models of masculinity and femininity, rather than cultural stereotypes

Battles with same-sex attraction are sometimes (though far from always) related to a sense of not quite measuring up to expected norms of what a man or woman is meant to be like. One of the factors that can lie behind same-sex attraction is actually fear of the same gender, a feeling of not quite belonging in maledom or femaledom. People of the same gender can seem to be somehow "other." So when the church reinforces superficial cultural stereotypes, the effect can be to worsen this sense of isolation and not quite measuring up. To imply that men are supposed to be into sports or fixing their own car, or that women are supposed to enjoy craft and to want to talk about everything, is to deal in cultural rather than biblical concepts. It may also actually end up overlooking many ways in which people are reflecting some of the biblical aspects of manhood and womanhood that culture overlooks.

5.2.5. Provide good pastoral support

Many churches run support groups for members who experience same-sex attraction; others provide mentoring or prayer-partner schemes. Pastoral care for those with same-sex attraction does not need to be structured, but it does need to be visible. Those with same-sex attraction need to know that the church is ready to support and help them, and that it has people with a particular heart and insight to be involved in this ministry. There may be issues that need to be worked through, and passages from the Bible that need to be studied and applied with care and gentle determination. There may be good friendships that need to be cultivated and accountability put in place, and there will be the need for long-term community. These are all things the local church is best placed to provide.

5.3. *For further reading*

Rosaria Champagne Buttterfield, *Secret Thoughts of a Reluctant Convert*, Pittsburgh: Crown and Covenant, 2012.
Sean Doherty, *The Only way is Ethics – Living Out My Story*, Authentic Media, 2015.
Andrew Goddard and Don Horrocks (eds), *Biblical and Pastoral Responses to Homosexuality*, Evangelical Alliance, 2012.
Ed Shaw, *The Plausibility Problem – The Church and Same-Sex Attraction*, IVP, 2015.
Alex Tylee, *Walking with Gay Friends*, IVP, 2007

If you have enjoyed this book, you might like to consider

- *supporting the work of the Latimer Trust*
- *reading more of our publications*
- *recommending them to others*

See www.latimertrust.org for more information.

LATIMER PUBLICATIONS

LATIMER PUBLICATIONS

Latimer Briefings

Anglican Foundations Series

Latimer Books

GGC	*God, Gays and the Church: Human Sexuality and Experience in Christian Thinking*	eds. Lisa Nolland, Chris Sugden, Sarah Finch
WTL	*The Way, the Truth and the Life: Theological Resources for a Pilgrimage to a Global Anglican Future*	eds. Vinay Samuel, Chris Sugden, Sarah Finch
AEID	*Anglican Evangelical Identity – Yesterday and Today*	J.I.Packer, N.T.Wright
IB	*The Anglican Evangelical Doctrine of Infant Baptism*	John Stott, Alec Motyer
BF	*Being Faithful: The Shape of Historic Anglicanism Today*	Theological Resource Group of GAFCON
TPG	*The True Profession of the Gospel: Augustus Toplady and Reclaiming our Reformed Foundations*	Lee Gatiss
SG	*Shadow Gospel: Rowan Williams and the Anglican Communion Crisis*	Charles Raven
TTB	*Translating the Bible: From William Tyndale to King James*	Gerald Bray
PWS	*Pilgrims, Warriors, and Servants: Puritan Wisdom for Today's Church*	ed. Lee Gatiss
PPA	*Preachers, Pastors, and Ambassadors: Puritan Wisdom for Today's Church*	ed. Lee Gatiss
CWP	*The Church, Women Bishops and Provision: The Integrity of Orthodox Objections to the Proposed Legislation Allowing Women Bishops*	
TSF	*The Truth Shall Set You Free: Global Anglicans in the 21st Century*	ed. Charles Raven
LMM	*Launching Marsden's Mission: The Beginnings of the Church Missionary Society in New Zealand, viewed from New South Wales*	eds. Peter G Bolt, David B. Pettett

LONG DRIVE SOUTH

Ten short stories

MARK BEASLEY

CONTENTS

COPYRIGHT

ABOUT THIS BOOK

From the publisher

Long Drive South is a collection of ten short stories based upon big ideas for as-yet unfinished novels. There's a laugh around every dark corner and a wicked twist to every tall tale.

Nothing is quite as it seems. A religious symbol takes on new meaning. A young woman meets her doppelganger. A sales rep has a life-changing experience. A new sausage is launched, with fatal consequences.

The cast list includes a dying rock star, a talentless writer, a homicidal business executive and five old friends at a terrifying school reunion.

If you appreciate good writing and dark humour, you will enjoy this book.

What readers say

"Mark Beasley wields a sharp pen and a mordant sense of humour."
- Christopher Somerville, author and Times journalist.

'Why has this comic genius only just started writing fiction?'
- Mary Killen, author, journalist and TV celebrity

"Deliciously twisted. Highly recommended."
- Steve Walwyn, musician and guitarist (Dr Feelgood)

"Dark, witty and insightful." M.L.

"A highly entertaining read...definitely recommended." S.M.

"Enjoyable and addictive...but strangely unsettling." P.W.

"Intriguing and well-written, with a sting in the tale." A.G.

"Each story is told with a delicious wickedness at its heart, a thumping twist in its tail and proper laugh-out-loud one-liners. If Beasley wrote this to prove he can write and entertain, he certainly doesn't disappoint."
- James Archer, writer

INTRODUCTION

First person at party: 'I'm writing a novel'

Second person at party: 'Really? Neither am I'

(Attributed to Peter Cook)

Thank you for reading my book. So far, so good.

Inspired by the great Peter Cook, I have written short stories that are based upon random ideas for the novel I have been failing to write.

A short story forces the writer to get to the point fast, to cut out all the filler and, preferably, to find an unexpected ending.

Along the way, I have sought cheap laughs wherever possible.

I hope you enjoy the book. If so, please let me know - and if you can, post a review on Amazon.

Mark Beasley
The Surrey Hills, UK
May 2021
www.markbeasley.net

LONG DRIVE SOUTH

STORIES I'VE TOLD

I

"After a career spent in Britain's hidden world of espionage and international crime, I have many stories to tell. Some of my secrets must go with me to my grave. And if I have done my job well, the stories I've told in this book will go with you to yours. I hope you enjoy them."

Colin Richards stops tapping at his keyboard and looks out of the window. His sixth sense was right. Rising quickly to his feet, he paces across the spare bedroom that he now calls his study and taps on the window: next door's cat is pissing on his vegetable patch again.

Turning back to the computer screen, he reads his work with pride. Perfect for the promotion page on Amazon and perhaps the fly sheet or cover of the book, he decides. Once he has got this sorted, his plan is to start writing the book itself. He reviews his description of the book.

"An exhilarating blend of intellectual intrigue, relentless adventure and biting wit, Colin Richards' book takes us on a masterful guided tour of Britain's secret services and their work. The plot is ferocious, the pace unforgiving and the lead character - Ric Collins - so gripping that I read the whole book in one sitting. The razor-sharp writing makes this the most exciting first novel in this genre to be published this year, if not this decade."

Richards sighs to himself. How can he possibly live up to his own hype? It turns out that writing a novel is not as easy as writing a scathing memo or email to one of the few people in his department weaker and less important than him.

Recently retired, he has spent most of his life commuting to his lowly civil service job in Westminster from his home in Carshalton - first a flat, then a terraced house, and now the semi that he shares with his wife, Valerie. Their children - Brian and Jane - left home a few years ago and are now doing something dull elsewhere in the suburbs. The apples have not fallen far from the tree.

The mortgage is finally paid off and with his Government pension, Colin feels secure enough to follow his passion - or he would, if he knew what it was. In the meantime, he's giving writing a go, using his son's old bedroom as a study, still adorned with posters of their one shared love - Crystal Palace Football Club.

To his family, and all who know him, Colin is a career pen-pusher, a time-serving dullard, finally collecting the pension that can surely have been his only ambition for all those years.

'Happy now?' he can hear them all thinking.

II

'Everyone thinks I'm just a boring old civil servant. Well, I'll show them', he'd told his wife, Valerie, over dinner one night.

'That's not strictly true,' she'd replied, 'You're actually a boring, retired, old civil servant.'

'That's what they think now. Wait until they read my book and find out who I really am.'

'Your book? What on earth will you put in a book? The day you lost your stapler? The time the photo-copier jammed?' She'd laughed and carried on with her crossword.

'Very funny. But I really have got some rather interesting stories to tell. Stories people haven't heard. Like the time I worked for MI5.'

Like all the best lies, there is a grain of truth in this. About twenty years ago, he had been co-opted from his job at the Department of Trade to work with M15 on an investigation.

Colin's main role had been to search for some old files, hidden deep in the bowels of Government, and then to write a report. A few phone calls and interviews were also involved, allowing him to revel in his 'MI5' persona.

'Not that old chestnut!' she'd laughed, again. 'You must have told everyone you know about it by now. And what about the Official Secrets Act?'

'That's why I'm writing it as a thriller. The main character won't be me, Colin Richards, but someone entirely different - Ric Collins, secret agent extraordinaire. That way I can mix fact with fiction: no-one will know which is which, but some of it will stick and add to my own glamour. Think of him as my *alter ego*.'

'Make *you* glamorous? No-one could ever be that good a writer! But I suppose that you of all people shouldn't find it too difficult to mix fact with fiction - you've been doing it for long enough. The stories you used to tell people - you practically made yourself out to be James Bond.'

'I'll admit that most of the stories I've told at parties and so on were indeed a pack of lies. But they were good lies - people enjoyed them. And that's all that matters to us writers.'

'They only said that to shut you up. But if that's what you want to do, carry on - it'll keep you out of my way. I'll give you a shout when the weather is better and then you can get outside and sort out the garden. That's if Hollywood hasn't snapped up the film rights by then.'

Colin retires to his study, where he continues not to write his novel.

III

Your lies can come back to haunt you, sometimes to kill you. Former Government Assassin Ric Collins is a man with a mysterious past and an uncertain future. A chance meeting forces him to confront his demons, leading to a winner-takes-all fight for everything he believes in. It will take all of Collins' experience, skills and cunning to get out of this - but his own words may be his worst enemy. Sometimes, even the darkest of secrets must see the light of day.

Colin stops and stares out of the window. He knows that promotional blurb and fake reviews are all part of the job these days, but he still hasn't started on the book itself.

However, he does have a legitimate excuse: he has no plot, no characters and no stories to tell, real or imagined. His mind is a complete blank, which was fine when he was pushing paper at his desk in the basement of the Department of Trade, but not for an aspiring novelist.

Let's face it, he thinks, I spent most of my career handling routine import and export administration and enquiries, tasks which required little or no wit or imagination, a requirement I was able to meet only too easily.

And then, when I was involved with something interesting, the MI5 project, I took no interest and did as little as possible. The fact is, the blank pages of this book are an accurate reflection of my mind, my career and probably my entire life, he concludes.

He has happier memories. He's told a few stories in the pub and at dinner parties, usually after a few drinks, although it was unclear whether anyone paid much attention. All were recycled from the crime and thriller books he has always read avidly, and which he knew most of his friends did not. For added authenticity, he sprinkled his stories with jargon garnered from those books - words like 'asset', 'spook' and 'tradecraft'.

He particularly favoured the cold-war period: Fleming and Le Carré were the masters, of course, but he also had a fondness for the 1960s sensibilities of Len Deighton and the writers of the Great American Blockbuster, like Ludlum and Clancy. Lee Child was in a league of his own, as was Ian Rankin in the pure crime genre – the closest to police procedurals that Colin cared to go.

More recently, he was a great admirer of Mick Herron. To create a character like Jackson Lamb - a foul-mouthed burnt-out spy with health and hygiene issues - was a real achievement.

With his love of drinking, smoking and farting, his misogyny and his mastery of sarcasm, Lamb was strangely relatable, even if all of these behaviours had been phased out of the office years ago, in Colin's experience.

These days, even farting in the workplace was likely to lead to an internal complaint about odour harassment, followed by wind awareness counselling and a flatulence training course.

At Colin's office, the only suggestion of any sort of individuality or rebellion had been exhibited after a few after-work drinks, or by the sheer persistence of the small team of dedicated smokers meeting outside by the bins. Once, a man in accounts had brought his pet parrot into the office. What was his name – Mills? Miller? Milligan? Colourful characters were few and far between in the Department of Trade. Perhaps that could be my starting point, thinks Colin.

His reverie is interrupted by Valerie, who storms into his study angrily, as she does at least half a dozen times a day. She is not happy about something and it's all Colin's fault.

'Do you think you could possibly knock before entering my study, Val?' he tentatively asks. 'I'm engaged in some pretty serious writing up here. It takes considerable powers of concentration to produce high-quality fiction and...'

'Don't be so ridiculous, Colin. You spend most of your time staring out of the window and the rest of it online shopping. It's all very well for you, scratching your arse up here all day, but some of us have a house to maintain and work to do. I can't do everything myself, you know.'

And so it is that Colin is issued with his instructions.

IV

Colin puts on his jacket and walks to the shops. Down Palmerston Avenue, along Beulah Park Drive and left into Churchill Way. After leaving Budgens, he walks to the paper shop, even though Budgens sell newspapers. The reason for this is soon obvious: Justina is on duty.

Although only employed to work part-time behind the counter, to all intents and purposes, Justina runs the shop - and more recently its post office - with an icy Baltic efficiency that Ahmed, the owner, can only stand back and admire.

She combines this with the looks of a porn star, at least two other jobs, and a part-time law degree course. As usual, Colin can think of nothing coherent to say to her but, despite the lack of evidence, is quietly confident that she finds him attractive.

His mind full of unlikely fantasies as he leaves the shop, he collides with a tall thin man, walking towards him while checking his phone. As always, Colin is quick to apologise.

'I'm terribly sorry, I wasn't paying attention and...'

They stop and look at each other, aware that they have met before, but unsure of the details.

'It's you, isn't it' says the tall thin man, speaking with a whining suburban accent. 'The secret agent. The bloke from MI5. The spook. I never forget a face. And it's not as if I often meet secret agents in my line of work - I'm only an accountant.'

Colin remembers now. During his 'MI5' assignment, he'd interviewed this man with regard to the accounts of a company under investigation.
It had been purely routine and had led nowhere. A few boxes had been ticked and a brief report submitted to his bosses at the real MI5.

The other man introduces himself, extending a gangling arm, 'My name's Meaden. Geoff Meaden. I'm just visiting a client over the road there. What about you?'

'Colin Richards. I live round here. I'm retired from the service now,' said Colin, thinking that 'the service' might imply MI5 without actually saying so. 'I'm busy writing a book about my experiences. You know, the stories I couldn't tell at the time, that sort of thing.'

'Anything in particular?' asks Meaden. 'I'm a big fan of thrillers.'

'Oh, you know, money laundering, drug trafficking, smuggling, tax evasion, prostitution. The usual sort of thing,' says Colin, floundering.

'Some of the things we discovered never got acted on at the time, so now's the chance to bring them to light. Perhaps my successors will pick up on them, you never know. I'd watch out if I were you!'

Meaden laughs. 'Like I said, I'm just an accountant. I only worked for the company for a few months. But I've always been curious - did you find out anything interesting as the result of our meeting?'

Colin thinks back to the interview. He'd only done a few, but even so, this one is memorable only because of the behaviour of Meaden's boss, who'd been incredibly rude on the phone. Meaden had attended at the last minute, after his boss had refused point blank to attend.

Colin could hear him on the phone now. 'If you think I'm going to waste my time filling in forms in your poxy little office, you can think again. I'll send over my office boy, and you're lucky I'm doing that.' He'd then slammed the phone down.

He replied to Meaden: 'I only really remember your boss – quite a character.' They had both laughed, recognising what that meant. Colin carried on.

'I don't remember too much else about our meeting or the investigations we conducted into your company, I'm afraid. Once my team and I finished our work, which often took us months of detailed investigation, it was all out of our hands - we passed it all to a team of forensic accountants. Top men they were - Price Waterhouse, that sort of thing. And women of course, mustn't forget my diversity training.'

This was all fantasy. Colin couldn't resist a good story, as usual, and was being unusually creative. In fact. he didn't have a team: he worked alone. There were no months of detailed investigation: after each meeting, he'd filled in a form and sent it to Complin, his contact at MI5. There was no crack team of forensic accountants, either - he was supposed to analyse all the financial data himself.

Colin, being a civil servant and naturally lazy, had only looked in detail at one in ten of the companies he 'investigated' and just skimmed through the rest. There had been no investigations or arrests, as far as he knew, and MI5 seemed to lose interest in the whole subject soon afterwards. He had received no response to the report he had submitted and, with his usual lack of curiosity, he hadn't followed it up.

However, Meaden seems to be impressed, so Colin carries on extemporising. He was on a roll now, using an imagination he barely knew he had. 'As I recall, a number of the reports we submitted led to criminal investigations and there were some high-profile arrests and convictions. All hush-hush of course. Not that I'm surprised - no fraud or money-laundering scam could possibly have survived the sort of detailed work that we used to do.'

Colin's roll continued. 'In fact, we uncovered so much incriminating stuff, there are still rooms full of people working their way through it to this very day. I'm hoping that my book will remind them of some of the juicier cases they're sitting on and bring them to light.'

'You've got me worried now,' says Meaden, laughing. 'Supposing my company had done something wrong - not that they had, obviously?'

'Oh you don't need to worry. They're only after the bosses - the organ grinders - not the monkeys, like you. Sorry, no disrespect.'

'None taken. I was just a trainee back then. But I'd be interested in your book - make sure you send me a signed copy. I want to see if my old boss is in it.'

On this jaunty exchange, they shake hands and Meaden walks off, leaving Colin pensive. The boss: what was his name again? Wilkinson? Watkins?

V

For decades, the Costa del Sol has been a playground for some of Europe's most dangerous criminal masterminds. At least fourteen UK-led crime firms are still based in the so-called Costa del Crime, enjoying the fruits of their ill-gotten gains. In his palatial luxury villa in the hills overlooking Marbella, a wronged man watches, waits and plots his revenge. Today, under the hot sun, he lost - but he'll be back, armed and dangerous.

Sitting on his terrace, Steve Wilkes puts down the paperback and reaches for his beer. The San Miguel is cold, the Spanish sun is shining and the sea is bright blue. Life is sweet.

In his sixties, Wilkes is wearing reasonably well. His greying wavy hair sits above a heavily suntanned, wrinkled face that resembles a fresh cowpat, from behind which his blue, twinkling eyes observe the world shrewdly, missing nothing.

Let's be clear about one thing: Steve Wilkes is not a wealthy criminal mastermind. Despite his best efforts, the cards just haven't fallen that way. Technically, he isn't even a criminal, as he has never been found guilty of anything. And even his best friend wouldn't call him a mastermind.

Wilkes isn't wealthy either, not anymore: he'd been involved in a few cock-ups, been screwed over a few times and had walked away from a few deals just ahead of the law.

But he had known when to cash in his chips and had settled for a comfortable, if not extravagant, life in the sun. He still had a few business interests and a good enough grasp of technology to stay on top of things. Life is indeed sweet.

No palatial villa with a pool either, but Steve is happy enough with the small, whitewashed house in the Andalucian hilltop village of Mojacar, with its terrace and distant sea view, that he shares with his third wife, Sonia.

Twenty years younger than Wilkes, she was even browner than he was, with the gold jewellery, bleached blond hair and designer clothing that were still fashionable in this part of the expat world. Years of lying in the sun had left her face less like a cowpat and more like a scrunched-up brown paper bag, often scaring people with the sun-damaged horror mask that emerged from beneath her immaculate blond bob.

Sonia walks onto the terrace, wearing a short white dress, bejewelled sandals and a knock-off Prada handbag. Powerful perfumes fill the air. 'Time to go, babes. We said we'd see Rob and Susanna at eight.'

They are meeting their friend Rob Kempton and his latest girlfriend for drinks and dinner at Desert Springs, a golf course that Wilkes belongs to and where Kempton has a villa (with a pool large enough to annoy Wilkes). The thatched clubhouse looks up to the mountains, with a carp-filled lake in front, filled with the distinctive fragrance of the Dama del Noche that grows up the walls.

Wilkes loves it. Golf clubs are his spiritual home and he is never happier than when seated at the bar, dressed like a large child in a designer polo shirt and tailored shorts, talking bollocks with a group of like-minded men, while their wives sat elsewhere, out of earshot.

Steve and Sonia are well-known in the area, especially in the golf clubs, bars and restaurants frequented by the large expat British community. The lucky few live in large villas in the mountains above Mojacar, in exclusive enclaves like La Parata.

But this is not Monaco, or even Marbella. Many other British ex-pats inhabit small holiday apartments in large blocks erected cheaply on waste ground near the village - so small in most cases that golf clubs and other possessions have to be kept in the boots of cars.

At the bottom of the social ladder, some expats survive in dilapidated housing developments inland, abandoned by rogue Spanish builders and without planning permission or connection to public utilities. So while Steve may not be Mr Big, he is certainly Mr Large and is satisfied with his status, even if he isn't in Kempton's league. As he assembles his wallet and car keys, his phone rings.

'I'd better just take this, love. Hello? Yes, that you Geoff?'

'Hi Steve, how's tricks? Sorted out that swing of yours yet?'

'I'm working on it, mate. When you're over next, I'll show you, we can play up at the club. Anyway, that isn't why you called, is it.'

'No, you're right. I thought I'd just give you the heads-up. I was down in Carshalton yesterday, seeing a client, when I bumped into a face from the past. Remember that MI5 bloke you made me go and see all those years ago?'

'Not really, no. What about him?'

'Well, he certainly made an impression on me. I was just a young lad at the time, so to go to a meeting with an MI5 agent in a basement in London was quite a big deal. They were doing some sort of investigation - routine, or so he said - and wanted to go through your books. I thought nothing more of it at the time, he didn't seem very interested and after flicking through the paperwork I gave him, we started talking about football. He's a Palace fan as I recall, and...'

'Get to the point, Geoff, get to the bloody point. I don't care if he's the manager of Manchester F*cking United, what's this got to do with me?'
'Well, it looks like he might have been doing a number on us.'

'A number? What the f*ck do you mean, Geoff.'

'Well it turns out that some of the best accountants in London have been crawling all over your paperwork and accounts, ever since. They're still working through all the cases they've got, one prosecution at a time. And now he's writing a book about it all, trying to shake things up.'

'F*ck me Geoff, what on earth are you on about? Who cares about some book? There was nothing in those accounts to worry anyone, let alone MI5. After all, you prepared them, didn't you.'

'Yes, I did' admitted Meaden. 'But I was only a trainee at the time. They're using Price Waterhouse now - they could easily work out what you're up to. This isn't the local old bill, Steve. No plumbing supplies business could ever be that profitable, let alone export to Spain - all the sizing is different, for a start. Metric and Imperial, that sort of thing.'

Wilkes went quiet. He could see that Meaden was right. It was only a relatively small amount of money every year, but he'd been doing it for decades. The money came over in the van, it was exchanged for weed shipped over from Morocco by a bloke he met in a local beach bar, which was hidden in copper piping and sent back to the UK. Easy money and not that much of it - but by now, it must add up to more than he could ever afford to pay back. Not to mention the fines and the possible jail sentence.

'Did this MI5 guy say anything else?'

'Just that they're looking into the whole lot: drug trafficking, extortion, money laundering, smuggling, tax evasion, prostitution…that sort of thing.'

'What sort of thing, you half-wit? Do they think I'm the bloody mafia or something? A bit of weed for some mates in exchange for pocket money and that's about it. They can't pin all that lot on me, surely. And as for prostitution.' Sonia gave all that up years ago, thinks Wilkes. But he's a worried man.

'OK, thanks Geoffrey. Leave it with me.'

VI

Ric Collins carries out his press-ups with military precision, mentally counting the number of times his chin touches her shoulder.

'Looks like another flat hair day tomorrow', the woman gasps, as his metronomic thrusts force the back of her head to repeatedly hit the headboard, sending fragments of wallpaper and plaster flying.

A covert late-night meeting with Natasha, a Russian agent, had been followed by a drink in Collins' hotel room and, inevitably, some epic lovemaking.

'Sorry, babe', he replies, reaching 100 and rolling onto his back whilst lifting her in the air. 'I forgot that you Russians always like to stay on top of things.'

'Making me do all the hard work, huh', she moans, while he lays back and checks his phone impassively, her long red hair falling over the screen as she bucks and writhes athletically.

'So now you don't you like the look of my face?', she groans, as Collins humps her skilfully from behind, balancing his entire bodyweight on one hand whilst doing so.

After their fourth coupling, she passes out. Collins pulls on his tracksuit and goes for a run. Now to work up a proper sweat.

Colin smiles and relaxes. This is great writing by any standards, he thinks. It's the only part of the actual book he has written so far and establishes the main character - and therefore by implication Colin himself - as a highly accomplished lover. He can already guess Valerie's comment on that one.

He's getting good at this, he thinks. Now all he has to do is to weave a book around this important passage. He just needs a plot, some characters and 100,000 more words. At his current rate of about 100 words a day, that's another three years, he realises - but things should speed up a fair bit once he's got the hang of it.

Then he's struck by self-doubt. Is it too under-stated? Should it be it more explosive or more detailed. Perhaps something a bit kinky is needed - games, toys, a gun or a mask?

Was the bed too old-fashioned as the location? He is imagining some additional scenarios, with Justina from the paper shop standing in for Natasha, as Valerie storms angrily into the room.

After a diatribe about something or other - Colin didn't listen to it all, but the gist of it seemed to involve a failed Sainsbury delivery - Colin is given his orders: a trip to the shops is required. Not now, but later. He carries on trying to write, praying for inspiration.

VII

High in the hills, above the stench, corruption and violence of the city, a group of old friends meet, as they have met every year for the past 30 years. Their mission: to hunt down one man - a man with the knowledge that could ruin all their lives - and to bring him to justice. Their sort of justice. They are now closer than ever before. This evening, after dark, he will be theirs. It will not be pretty. It will not be fair. And they will savour every visceral moment.

The sun is low over the mountains as Steve Wilkes drives his elderly Jag through the security barrier - which has been unmanned for at least ten years, to his certain knowledge - and pulls up in the member's car park at Desert Springs. It's still warm, and he stops to relish the heady scent of flowers and the restrained tweeting of birds. Don't ask me which birds or flowers, he thinks, I'm not David Attenborough. But one thing's for sure - you don't get closer to nature than a golf course. Sonia pulls her white jacket over her shoulders and they walk into the clubhouse.

Kempton and Susannah are waiting at the bar, festooned in designer labels, reeking of name-brand fragrances and with expensive-looking drinks in front of them. Kisses and handshakes are exchanged.

'Ah, Wilkes. There you are at last. I thought you two weren't coming. We were about to give up and go home, weren't we, Susie?'

'Sorry we're a bit late, Rob. I got a call from my accountant back in the UK just as we were leaving. Took me a while to shut him up so we could get over here.'

'Only joking, old chap. Now, what are you drinking? And let's have a look at the menu while we're at it.' He makes hand gestures and a waiter appears from nowhere, menus in hand, while the barman prepares their drinks. Kempton is a man who makes things happen.

'Now then Paco, what's good this evening?' he asks the waiter, as he always does. 'Gambas de Garrucha - excellent. And lubina – that's sea bass, isn't it? Sounds good to me - how about the rest of you?'

Food ordered, a second round of drinks underway, and Wilkes is a slightly less worried man. Rob Kempton has that effect on people - tanned, groomed and confident, he is everything that Steve is not, and considerably wealthier.

In Kempton's world, worries are optional and anything is possible. It may not always be legal, but it is always possible. You get to know the right people, you groom them, you take what you want and give them what they want - usually money.

'Rob, can I ask you something? It's a bit delicate.'

'Fire away, old chap. My usual charges apply.'

'Well, it looks like I may be the subject of an MI5 enquiry, all because some dickhead of a retired agent is writing a book - some sort of exposé, apparently.'

Kempton smiled. 'You? MI5? Are you sure about this? You're not exactly Blofeld, are you. I'd have thought the local plod on his bike was more your level.'

'My plumbing supplies business got chosen for a random audit bloody years ago and it turns out that ever since then, they've had teams of people working their way through the findings. All I've ever done is to smuggle a bit of weed back to some mates in Kent, but now they're talking about extortion, drug trafficking, money laundering, smuggling, tax evasion, prostitution…you name it.'

'Prostitution?' says Kempton, glancing at Sonia - he has previous experience there, back when she was on the game. Not too bad, as he recalls. 'It all seems a bit unlikely, Steve. Well, most of it, anyway. How do you know this?'

'My accountant, Geoff Meaden, bumped into the guy. He was full of himself, apparently. Talked about all the stories he could tell, now that he was retired. Not to mention all the information that MI5 had, just waiting to see the light of day. It made me a little nervous, I can tell you.'

'Meaden? That long streak of piss. Why on earth are you still using him? I introduced you to my guy years ago - he's saved me an absolute fortune in tax and can be quite creative, if you know what I mean.'

'Geoff isn't the sharpest tool in the box, I'll grant you. But he's trustworthy and his rates are low - and for someone like me, that's important.'

'Bloody hell Wilkes, you cheapskate. No wonder you're still living in that rat-infested shanty of yours up in Mojacar. Anyway, how can I help?'

'I thought you might know someone who could have a word with this guy - Colin Richards he's called - and persuade him to back off. He must have plenty of other mugs he can write about, without mentioning me.'

'Have a word? What do you mean exactly?' asked Kempton. 'Threats? Extreme violence? Cut him into pieces, roll him up in a carpet and chuck him into a lake? Not exactly my sort of thing, Steve, you should know that.'

'Well, I suppose I meant just that - have a word. A couple of scary hardmen, an implied threat. That's all that's needed, I'd have thought. Although now you come to mention it, maybe it will take more than that to shut this guy up.'

'As it happens, I do have a couple of blokes in cloaks back in the UK I sometimes use to chase up bad debts for me, that sort of thing,' said Kempton, keeping his voice low so their wives didn't hear.

'Very scary indeed, they are. And I believe they'll go a lot further than threats if the price is right - a lot further. Or so I'm told - I've never done anything like that myself, you understand. Would that help?'

'That would be absolutely brilliant, Rob. Let me think about it and I'll give you a call tomorrow with the details.'

'No problem. Just let me know what you want doing. Now, shall we go and sit at our table?'

VIII

Ric Collins, a suave, wise-cracking, globe-trotting analyst turned agent is asked to investigate some of Europe's largest criminal enterprises. Ten years later, Collins is forced to re-think everything. He's enjoyed being in the game, but now the rules are changing, fast. And he's not sure he wants to play anymore.

As he walks towards his fashionable home in London's bohemian Carshalton district, he is unaware of the black van following him, its lights turned off. Instead, he is thinking of his new Eastern European lover and what they will be doing later that evening.

'That's him,' says the passenger to the driver, who slows the van to a halt. Putting on a balaclava, the passenger jumps out, grabs the pedestrian

from behind and puts a gloved hand over his mouth, before throwing him into the back of the van.

'I made it all up. I don't know anything. I'm just a boring civil servant' shouts Collins, as everything goes dark.

Colin is a happy man. He is walking to the shops again, as requested: down Palmerston Avenue, along Beulah Park Drive and left into Churchill Way. It's a warm evening and he has a spring in his step, as he has managed to write another 150 words. Good words, maybe even great words.

He reviews them while they're still fresh in his mind. *Wise-cracking*; he likes that: a hero with a fast mind, a quick wit and an appreciation of irony. That extended riff on being in the game - fellow-writers will admire what he's done there. However, he may have to work on the locality, as Carshalton may not be quite right. Docklands perhaps?

But the denouement, when Ric Collins is thrown into the van - that's right up there with any modern thriller. Who knows what these hired killers will do to Collins now: whatever it is, it won't be pretty. Should he describe the violence in bloody detail, or leave it to the reader's imagination?

As Colin turns into Churchill Way, he thinks about Justina in the paper shop. Should he tell her that he had her in mind when writing the sex scenes? He imagines her surprise and pleasure: she's bound to be flattered, maybe even overawed. But however aroused and available she is, what could he do about it? Val knows his every move.

Colin realises that life would be so much easier - and infinitely more enjoyable - if he could move between fact and fiction, as and when it suited him. Move over Ric Collins, it's time for suave, wise-cracking, sex-God Colin Richards to step out of the shadows. Time for the stories I've told to become reality.

Lost in his own words, he doesn't notice the black van slowing to a halt behind him.

DOUBLE CROSS

I

Nigel Ashley wakes up with a start. He swivels his balding gingery head and looks around the aircraft angrily, his red face showing barely concealed contempt for all that he sees. His default expression, thinks Susan, his wife.

The in-flight announcement that had disturbed him continues. 'We will shortly be commencing our final descent into Lorca International Airport, Murcia. BudJet would like to thank you for choosing to travel with us today.'

'Thank God', says Nigel. 'The sooner I'm out of this hellhole and away from all these plebs, the happier I'll be. It was bad enough getting up at half-past three in the morning, without having to slum it with this rabble.'

'Don't be such a dreadful snob, Nigel', says Susan. She's small, mousy and rarely speaks badly of anyone. In fact, she rarely speaks at all. What she is thinking, if anything, nobody really knows. 'She's probably a murderer on the quiet', jokes Nigel at dinner parties. She doesn't deny it, either.

'But I must admit that Quick Boarding isn't exactly Emperor Class, like our trip to the Maldives last year', she says.

Her husband nods in agreement. Yes, that was more like it. Young Asiatic hostesses in silk kimonos and saris, or whatever they were called, had smiled at his every word and anticipated his every need. Well, almost every need, he thinks, lapsing into an unsavoury fantasy.

Nigel flies regularly on business and has never had to pay for his own food and drink before, like today. And he has certainly never had his meal served in a brown paper bag and thrown to him over the heads of other passengers, either. His humorous attempt at barking and clapping like a seal in response had fallen flat, too.

However, this is the only way to get to the La Manga Club, where they will be joining a group of friends from their Hertfordshire village.

But for Nigel, there's a cloud on the horizon. It's their 22nd wedding anniversary - you serve less time for murder these days, jokes Nigel predictably - and Susan has arranged for the two of them to stay for two nights somewhere the other side of Murcia, before joining their friends.

'Where's that bloody place we're staying again?' asks Nigel.

'For goodness sake' replies Susan, looking up from her Eyewitness Guide. 'You never show any interest, do you. It's called the Parador de Las Dos Cruces. I showed you the website. The spa looks amazing. It's near Caravaca de la Cruz - a beautiful historic town that's famous for its cross, apparently. In the guidebook it says that 'the iconic double-armed cross is legendary for its healing power and ability to ward off evil spirits.' It all looks absolutely lovely - and so romantic.'

Nigel shudders and makes a despairing noise, like a man going down for the third and last time. Romantic? There's probably not even a golf course. And historic? In his experience, gained over many years of his wife's holiday choices, that usually meant stumbling around heaps of dusty rubble in the baking sun, while trying to look interested, as a guide drones on interminably and then tries to stiff you for a tip when he or she finally shuts up.

And Susan knows what she can do with her bloody double cross, or whatever it was she was going on about. Healing power? Evil spirits? Please, give me a break, he thinks.

As for the spa, trust his wife to find somewhere where she could spend most of the day shuffling around in a fluffy white bathrobe, spending his money on massages and treatments. It's not as if she's up for anything afterwards - she usually just falls asleep, pink and plump, her mouth open, with bits of seaweed and mud stuck in her hair.

The plane lands and they start to disembark. Some passengers have obviously been planning for a swift exit and push forward, but Nigel gains great satisfaction from getting in their way as much as possible, while surreptitiously kicking ankles and treading on a few feet. Bloody plebs.

He retrieves their bags from the overhead locker, ensuring they hit a few people on their way down, and makes a great show of ushering Susan into the gangway before they shuffle down the aisle.

The Spanish heat hits them as they walk down the aircraft steps. Putting on their sunglasses, they pull their cabin bags behind them and cross the road to enter the terminal building, fumbling for their passports.

Lorca Airport is large, modern and almost entirely devoid of facilities, passengers and aircraft. It looks like it was finished that morning (in fact, large parts of it are still unfinished, notes Nigel with grim satisfaction) and the building echoes as they walk through it.

Despite there being no other flight arrivals that morning, their luggage takes a long time to arrive. To pass the time, Nigel provides Susan, and anyone else within earshot, with a valuable tutorial on the inefficiency and incompetence of Spanish business in general and this airport in particular.

Eventually, their bags appear and, somehow balancing their suitcases and golf clubs on a trolley, they head for the car rental offices outside the terminal.

'Please don't tell me you booked GoCar again', says Nigel. 'You know I get a good corporate rate with Avis.'

'I did actually', says Susan, 'the GoCar rate was very reasonable and their cars are always so nice and clean. Anyway, Avis don't even have an office on the airport - there's only GoCar, Tonto or AutoRentals.'

'But good grief woman. GoCar! Check the internet, read Trip Advisor. Ten thousand one-star reviews can't be wrong - and they're the better ones. At best they're rip-off merchants, at worst they're crooks. They're legendary for their hidden charges, scams and rudeness. If you don't buy their extortionate additional insurance, they'll find some hidden damage when you return the car and then charge you a fortune for it. Last year, they even held a couple hostage until they paid up. It was in the papers!'

'You could always have booked it yourself, smart arse,' mumbles Susan to herself, surprising Nigel by striding off towards the rental car office.

'Wait here with the luggage and I'll go and sort the car out', she calls over her shoulder.

He takes a seat outside the terminal, muttering angrily to himself. Still, it is pleasantly warm and the view towards the mountains most acceptable. He pulls the latest Jack Reacher out of his bag and starts reading. Jack is busy breaking arms and busting heads.

That's my idea of customer feedback, thinks Nigel, fantasising about wreaking extreme violence upon a room full of car rental reps, budget airline executives and airport managers. He likes nothing better than taking offence at imaginary slights or insults and dozes off happily.

He is woken by Susan, tooting the horn of a shiny black Seat Arteca SUV. They've obviously been upgraded. He loads the luggage and takes over the driver's seat, as is his right.

'At least we've got some nice wheels', he comments, deciding that a small morsel of praise thrown her way might keep Susan quiet for a while. 'That rep you were talking to must have liked you. He looked a bit like that smarmy bloke who runs the Tapas bar in the village, Juan Cruz. He knows how to rip off his customers too.'

'I suppose he does a bit, says Susan, adjusting her sunglasses. 'But hasn't Juan got a moustache?'

Nigel makes a typically scathing - and to him, deeply satisfying - remark about his compete lack of interest in the facial hair arrangements of Spaniards, before pulling away and fiddling with the satnav. They circle the airport complex twice before finding the exit leading to the A7 motorway.

Standing outside the GoCar office, a lone figure watches them drive away.

II

'This is freaking awesome,' pronounces a loud American accent, cutting through the peace and beauty of the hotel courtyard like a chainsaw.

And it is, thinks Susan. The view was stunning, looking across a steep gorge to the ancient town of Caravaca de la Cruz, perched on the side of a mountain. According to her guidebook, El Parador de Las Dos Cruces was built on the site of a thirteenth century castle, once owned by a man with one of the best names in Spanish history - Pedro the Cruel. You knew where you stood in those days, thinks Susan. History is best when written in black and white.

They'd arrived at the Parador at midday and checked in. To Nigel's surprise - and slight annoyance, as he was hoping for an argument with the reception staff - their room was ready. After a quick freshen-up, they were now drinking coffee in the courtyard, shaded from the baking sun by jacaranda trees. A fountain is playing its watery music in the background.

It would be a lot more peaceful without the American and his companion, thinks Nigel. Although the other side of the courtyard, the loud male voice has been relentless.

'Bloody septics, always shooting their mouths off', comments Nigel, predictably. Just like his Father, thinks Susan, keeping one ear on the American while Nigel reads the English newspaper he'd picked up at the airport.

The American was on a roll. 'I mean, this place beats even Rennes Le Chateau for religious mystery. Hell, even Dan freaking Brown would be able to see that - who knows, if we're not careful he might write one of his godawful books about it some day.'

He pauses and takes a swig of his beer. 'And can you believe that the Pope made this town the fifth Holy City of Catholic Christianity in 1998? I mean - Rome, Jerusalem…and Caravaca de la Cruz! The goddamn Pope! A Holy freaking City!'

He throws himself back into his seat in stunned disbelief. He's tall and obviously used to talking, decides Susan. Probably about fifty and quite vain, with bleached blond hair, a tan and gleaming white teeth.

His female companion seems to be paying him as little attention as it is possible to do without being asleep. She is probably quite a few years younger, decides Susan. Hiding behind a straw hat and sunglasses, she is wearing tight white jeans and is holding a cigarette in one hand and a glass of wine in the other.

She seems effortlessly elegant and stylish to Susan, who feels more than a little suburban and drab by comparison. Which let's be fair, she is, as Nigel would happily confirm.

Instead, he raises his head from his newspaper to offer one of his regular unsolicited current affairs bulletins. 'This bloody Government. Old Farage has got the right idea, as usual. What they should do is …'.

Susan tunes out and continues listening to the American.

'And the Basilica of Vera Cruz. That's it, right at the top there. Would you believe they've got a cross in there that's believed to be made from the True Cross - the one that Jesus Freaking Christ himself was nailed to. It was guarded by the Knights Templar for eight centuries. This I have got to see.'

He reaches for his camera and takes some shots of the town. Most of these include his own grinning face - a technique he seems to have mastered, which involves holding the camera at arms-length whilst baring his dazzling teeth. He checks the results, pronounces them to be 'freaking awesome' and sits down.

This prompts Nigel to stand up, folding his paper noisily as he does. 'Let's go in and have some lunch, Sue. I've had more than enough of this idiot.'

He leads the way to the restaurant, followed reluctantly by Susan. But it's a beautiful space, she discovers, with a vine-covered patio, crisp white tablecloths and some of those reassuringly competent waiters that you only seem to find in Spain. Not too haughty, like the French, not too familiar, like the Italians.

Racial stereotypes can be so comforting, thinks Susan, feeling pleasantly relaxed as she sips her cava and looks contentedly at the loudmouthed American, still talking in the distance.

After some delicious fish and a cold bottle of Albariño, even Nigel is pleasantly relaxed, his mood not noticeably changing when the two Americans enter the restaurant and are seated at the next table. Susan - finding once again that only alcohol enables her to unleash the social animal hidden deep within - turns and speaks to them, slightly gabbling her words in her nervousness.

'Excuse me. I couldn't help overhearing what you were saying about the town earlier and I'd really like to know more. I haven't seen many holy cities - or true crosses, come to that.'

The American swivels in his chair with a massive smile on his face. He likes nothing better than an audience. Introductions take place, during which he is revealed as Dale Lincoln, a Brighton-based writer and presenter of esoteric historical mysteries on television.

The female - it's not clear if she is his wife or not, much to Susan's annoyance - is called Karyl. She is tall, slim and blonde, her white jeans concealing long elegant legs, which compare all too favourably with Susan's own trotters, as Nigel calls them.

Lincoln's interests, about which he is happy to talk at some length, include subjects like Atlantis, Crop Circles, King Arthur, Pyramids and Stone Circles, as well as many more obscure subjects which he recounts too quickly for Susan and Nigel to understand, let alone remember.

He is nothing if not an enthusiast, requiring little in the way of encouragement, and his approach seems refreshingly open-minded, in that no idea or discovery is too ludicrous or unfounded to be legitimised by his own appraisal. At one point, he refers to a conversation he once had with a 'man from the future', causing even Karyl to look confused and irritated.

Nigel is quick to despise Lincoln's unlimited enthusiasm, deploying every critical tool at his disposal, from irony and sarcasm to attempts at intellectual engagement. But Lincoln is impervious to anything which disrupts his own stream of consciousness and Nigel's carefully-honed interventions wither and die during Lincoln's lengthy discourse.

'You can't argue with a true believer,' he tells Susan later, adding his own satisfyingly concise analysis: 'That bloody Yank really does talk a load of five-star bollocks.'

Karyl seems to take little interest in any of this and is clearly only here for the ride. And the drink, notes Susan bitchily - don't think I haven't seen how many she's had. However, she has to admit that permanent inebriation is probably the best response to Dale's never-ending stream of nonsense.

Refreshed by a few mouthfuls of coffee (and surely he is no stranger to other, more exotic, stimulants, thinks Nigel) Lincoln has moved up a gear and is talking about his greatest enthusiasm, which he describes as the 'mystery and enigma' of a place called Rennes Le Chateau.

It all washes over Nigel, who has had a few drinks himself by now: something about an obscure French village, a priest and the bloodline of Christ himself, he thinks.

This is the reason that Lincoln is here, it turns out: there may be a connection with Caravaca de la Cruz. More importantly, there could well be a television programme to be made, presented by Dale Lincoln, international man of mystery and all-purpose conspiracy expert.

'There's definitely more to Caravaca being awarded Holy City status than meets the eye,' asserts Lincoln. 'I mean, they built a seventy-mile motorway from Murcia to Caravaca de la Cruz, a small town in the middle of nowhere. A motorway that is usually deserted. Why does the Pope have to get here that quickly? Can't the Popemobile travel on ordinary roads?'

Caravaca de la Cruz is indeed a place of considerable mystery, explains Lincoln. A town named after a cross - and not just any cross, but the one that Christ died on - and the site of miracles and visitations by angels. It is quite amazing that so few British tourists come here, given its amazing myths and history, he says - clearly inviting us to agree that they are all morons, thinks Susan. And he's right, why would you lie on the beach when you could be exploring somewhere like this?

Caravaca even has its own logo - a double cross, or to be more precise, a heraldic two-barred cross consisting of a vertical line crossed by two shorter horizontal bars. Unlike most logos, this is a symbol rich in 'historical significance, devotional potency, and practical ritual power'.

Lincoln is able to reel off phrases like this to order, notes Susan. Which is quite impressive really. This is the cross at the top of the Basilica, which itself is at the very top of the town.

Despite Lincoln's revelations, Nigel can hardly contain his boredom and scepticism. However, Susan looks more animated than he has seen her look since their neighbours got a new dog or her Mother bought new curtains.

Karyl lights another cigarette and drinks more wine, her expression impenetrable and her jeans barely concealing her more feminine charms, attracting Nigel's lustful gaze.

But Lincoln has hardly drawn breath, moving on to talk about freemasonry, the Illuminati, the Knight's Templars and satanism, his enthusiasm and love for himself and his subject matter increasing with each sentence.

'Hey, we're going there tomorrow, why don't you guys join us? I've just got to find someone to drive us and a local guide. I always like to have a local guide, they're so authentic,' concludes Dale.

'I'd really love that' says Susan, 'it's all absolutely fascinating. I love the double cross thing. My mind is positively whirring.'

Karyl pats her arm 'That's real nice of you, Sue, but please don't feel you have to encourage all his bullshit. Mind you, it would be nice to have some sane company for a change.' She jerks her thumb at Dale and takes another mouthful of wine.

Nigel says that regrettably, he's unable to join them, almost sounding as though he means it, but would be very happy to drive them all there and back. He is thinking of finding a quiet bar somewhere and enjoying a relaxing beer or three.

Welcome to Caravaca de la Cruz, the home of the double cross, thinks Susan. Her mind was indeed whirring.

III

The next morning, Nigel is eating breakfast alone, sitting in the shade outside the restaurant, reading a newspaper. One thing you can say about the Spanish, he concedes grudgingly, they make bloody good coffee.

Susan had got up before him, something about popping into the village. Who cares, he reasons, it gives me a bit of peace and quiet - much needed after the drinks he had consumed in the bar the night before, after Susan had gone to bed.

He had met a group of golfers in the bar and one thing had led to another. In fact, it had been three in the morning before he staggered back to their room, unsure of who had bored whom the most.

The golfers had reminded Nigel that he was looking forward to seeing the gang from home in a few days. The Brancasters, Paul and Jane Duke, The Burtons, Peter and Ann Washington, even John and Pam Roberts, who had made a fortune in IT and were much admired. And a few others too dull (the men) or too ugly (the wives) to even think about, but who would provide a willing audience for Nigel and the other alpha males in the group.

The men would play golf and, after dinner, stay in the bar till late. Here, they would drink too much, discuss cars, tell jokes and guffaw loudly at any and every opportunity. It was all a little like Top Gear (Clarkson era, obviously), but without the wit, intelligence or political correctness.

Meanwhile, the women would play tennis, sunbathe, compare notes on the many achievements of their children (and increasingly, grandchildren) and try to trump each other with tales of household purchases, restaurants and holidays.

They too would drink too much and shriek with fake indignation and laughter as they did so, although none of them ever said anything remotely funny. Even Susan managed to get a few squeaks in once she was with that lot, thought Nigel.

Susan returns from whatever it was she had been doing in the village and slams her bag on the table, blowing Nigel's paper to the floor in the process. It's probably full of unnecessary trinkets, magazines and unguents, thinks Nigel, as he theatrically retrieves his paper from the floor.

'The wretched car's playing up', she announces. 'I've arranged for someone from GoCar to come and have a look at it while we're parked in the town later. That means we won't have to wait around for them here all day.'

Trust the bloody Spanish, thinks Nigel. He can't be bothered to ask for more information. His opinion of rental car companies and their employees, particularly the Spanish ones, is extremely low anyway, so he is not at all surprised at this latest turn of events.

However, it's a shame not to wheel out a few oven-ready caustic remarks on the subject, so he does, interrupting Susan, who is still explaining the arrangements she has made. Nigel is at his worst when taking minor incidents and elaborating on them *ad nauseam,* as he does now.

'So first they make you wait in a queue for hours while they fiddle with their hopelessly slow computers. It's not as if they don't know you're coming, for God's sake. How many times have we used GoCar – and we still have to give them our bloody life story every time we stand at one of their desks. Then they give you a bloody death trap to drive around in - remember that one with no steering? And if you're still alive when you return the car, they fleece you for as much as they can get away with, knowing you're in a hurry to catch your flight.'

Susan looks at Nigel blankly, her thoughts known only to herself. To maintain this façade, which hides years of pent-up anger, bitterness and hatred, she toys with a souvenir she has bought - a wooden double cross - as though it were a rosary. She pours herself a cup of coffee, as Dale and Karyl appear.

Dale has carried out more research overnight. He is now convinced that the key to the mystery lies not in the Basilica itself, at the top of the town, where all the pilgrims and tourists go, but in a small Church – the Church of El Salvador - which lies further down the hill and may contain tunnels leading directly underneath the Basilica.

In fact, the whole place is riddled with ancient tunnels, he says, providing a sort of metro system underneath the town.

The Priest who witnessed the first miraculous appearance of the cross was rumoured to have spent time there, in meditation and prayer. And the Pope was believed to have made a private visit when he visited the town in 1998.

Dale pauses. 'So for some reason, they still celebrate mass down there. Or maybe hold more sinister rituals – who knows? This I have got to see.'

Susan smiles, exposing her imperfect, yellowing teeth to Nigel's contemptuous gaze.

'I've got some good news' she announces, 'I was down in the village and the shopkeeper put me onto a local guide. He's available this afternoon or evening and can meet us over there if we call him to agree a time.'

Dale pronounces this to be awesome news and orders them all coffee. 'That's great', says Karyl to Susan, who takes her to another table, where they talk quietly.

Nigel rustles his newspaper noisily and carries on reading, his mind full of contempt for Dale. Why does he think his presence at a historical site is so important? The site has been there for hundreds if not thousands of years, happily minding its own business, yet this self-educated moron, his head full of crap and drivel, thinks he can show up and validate ancient mysteries just by being there.

IV

It's early evening. The sun is low in the sky, it's still warm and everyone is feeling good after lunch and a siesta by the pool.

Susan has sunbathed a little, self-consciously wearing her new swimming costume, while Nigel has read his Jack Reacher book. She has much to be self-conscious about, notes Nigel, comparing her flabby, freckly body with Karyl's rather more streamlined version, now showcased in a white one-piece. They've agreed to drive over to Caravaca de la Cruz, do the guided tour, and return for a late dinner (as if there is any other sort in Spain, thinks Nigel).

The car crosses the narrow bridge that takes them over the steep gorge. From here, the town is approached by a steep curving road leading to the old town and its Plaza, where there is a path up to the Basilica, perched at the very top.

Nigel drops the other three at the bottom of the hill, close to the Church of El Salvador, where the guide is waiting outside. He then drives up the hill to the Plaza, parks the car as agreed and heads off to find a decent bar. The car seems fine to him, but he's buggered if he's going to hang around waiting to discuss it with the GoCar chap. Susan has presumably told him the problem and he's bound to have a key, he reasons.

After a few false starts, Nigel finds a bar he likes the look of. Called El Cid, it has a few tables out front, looking onto a small square with trees and a fountain. Groups of young people and older couples with small dogs walk by, enjoying their *paseo*.

Inside, the bar is bright with harsh neon light, an ambience enhanced by the scrunched-up napkins all over the floor and the usual group of unfriendly locals in short-sleeved shirts.

So far, so Spanish, thinks Nigel. They are all watching a television, fixed to the wall at ceiling height, playing a football match at high volume.

Real Madrid seem to be beating some team Nigel hasn't heard of, so he decides to take a seat outside. An attractive young waitress takes his order: he covertly stares at her breasts while fixing her with what he mistakenly believes to be an irresistible smile.

The beer is cold and the tapas surprisingly edible, even if he hadn't known what he was ordering. The tables have filled up with groups of local people who are talking loudly, usually at the same time.

Soft lighting is hidden in the gardens, sneaking up the side of the palm trees as dusk arrives. The air is fragrant with tobacco smoke and perfume. Nigel feels inexplicably happy and orders another beer. Life is pretty bloody good really, he thinks.

V

Susan, Dale and Karyl meet the guide, a moustachioed Spaniard, outside the church. He introduces himself formally, shaking hands with Dale and kissing the hands of Susan and Karyl, before addressing them in accented but fluent English.

'Welcome to Caravaca de la Cruz and the Church of El Salvador. My name is Juan Cruz - yes, that's John Cross in English, well done Señor – and it will be my pleasure to introduce you to some of the secrets of this wonderful town. But first, I wonder whether we could deal with the small matter of payment.'

Dale happily hands Juan a bundle of notes, making sure he has added a large tip: he comes from Chicago and this is in his DNA.

Juan leads them round the side of the Church, rough brick and stonework on one side, dusty wasteland rising steeply towards the Plaza on the other. They stop at a small side door, which Juan opens with a large rusty key, theatrically ushering them inside.

They enter what seems to be a basement, containing nothing of interest other than broken chairs and a pile of dogeared bibles. Dale, however, pronounces the room to be 'awesome' and photographs everything, from all possible angles.

At the far end of the basement, Juan opens a trapdoor. He turns on a light, revealing a stepladder, leading downwards. They all descend, with Juan a bit too familiar with Susan, thinks Karyl, as he helps her down. It's almost as though they know each other, although she does not know how this could be possible: Susan only arrived yesterday and said that she had never been here before.

At the bottom, they enter a long corridor, with rough concrete walls and floor. Dale strides off ahead, disappearing from view as he turns a corner.

'Hey guys, this is a dead end,' he announces, his voice echoing around the walls, 'Juan, where's the entrance to these frigging tunnels?'

Instead of answering, Juan climbs back up the stepladder, followed by Susan. They slam the trapdoor shut, lock it and run.

Dale's muffled voice follows them. 'You double-crossing Spanish bastard. Let us out of here. I want my money back.'

His voice fades away as Susan and Juan run up the steep footpath, away from the Church and towards the Plaza, the golden two-barred cross at the top of the Basilica silhouetted against the orange sky.

'That's them out of the way', says Susan, 'The less they see, the better. That bloody American puts everything onto the internet within seconds, usually with his own gurning face at the front of the shot, and we really don't need that sort of exposure.'

On the other side of the town, Nigel finishes his third beer and pays his bill, leering one last time at the waitress. He strolls back to the car, enjoying the bustle and smells of a warm Spanish evening. Plenty of time to get down the hill to pick up the others, he thinks, as he opens the car door, climbs in and starts the engine.

Back at the Church, Dale has managed to open the trapdoor. He and Karyl are now walking up the winding side roads leading from the church, which he thinks will take him to the very top of the town, to the Basilica. He is almost incoherent with rage.

'What the hell. What the actual hell. There weren't even any tunnels. He just locked us in and ran.'

'Sorry Babe,' says Karyl. 'She just wanted us out of the way for a while.'

'You knew about this?' says Dale.' 'You knew they were planning to lock us in the basement of a church?'

'Like I say, she just wanted us out of the way and I went along with it. There's something going on, I don't know what, and she didn't want us to see it.'

'She thinks you're too damn inquisitive, for one thing, Dale - especially the way you photograph absolutely everything in sight and then post it on social media. Maybe whatever it is, she just doesn't want the whole world to know about it.'

'You should have asked her for more details,' he says, speeding up. 'I suppose you were too drunk - again. Anyway, they haven't seen the last of me yet.'

'I was not drunk. Well, only a little. Just because I know how to enjoy myself instead of boring everyone rigid with all your ridiculous conspiracy nonsense, like you. Mind you, there's definitely something going on - she knew that Juan guy, for sure.'

They reach the Basilica, which commands a spectacular view of the town and the countryside below it, now hazy and red as the sun disappears over the horizon. They lean against the perimeter wall and look down the cliff face to the Plaza, the steep winding road down the mountain and the deep gorge below.

Dale nudges Karyl. 'Look – there she is.'

Susan is standing at a viewpoint above the Plaza, between two tall men with dark hair. One is Juan, their guide, whose arm is around Susan, her head leaning on his shoulder. The other man, who has a moustache, is wearing overalls emblazoned with the GoCar logo. All three are watching the car park intently.

'You're right', says Dale. 'Something is going on, for sure. I knew he was no guide - I asked him about the Priory of Sion and he just looked at me blankly. I'll bet Nigel doesn't know a thing about any of this.'

Nigel has now driven out of the Plaza and joined the road leading downhill. He is not happy, either. It turns out that there is something wrong with the car, after all, although for some reason he hadn't spotted it on the way up. And whatever it is, the GoCar guy has not fixed it.

Bloody typical, he thinks, perking up a little at the thought of the choice words and extensive bollocking he would dispense later that evening. Meanwhile, the car is picking up speed. The brakes seem a little spongy, as Nigel puts his foot on the pedal. In fact, they're really not working at all well. Bloody Spanish.

A little worried now, he pumps the brake pedal frantically but to little effect. The brakes are now losing power, as with each pump, brake fluid is ejected from new holes in the brake hoses. The car picks up speed as it approaches a sharp bend.

Nigel spins the wheel, stamping on the increasingly ineffective brake pedal, while changing to a lower gear. The engine squeals and the tyres screech as he catches a glimpse of his wife, canoodling with the guy who runs the local tapas bar back home.

Bloody Juan Cruz, the bastard. And the other guy - he was at the car rental office. You rat-faced double-crossing little bitch, he thinks, as the brakes fail altogether and he loses control of the car.

'It's so lovely to see your hometown at last, Juan,' says Susan. 'And to meet your brother, too.'

The Cruz brothers. Double Cross. This is indeed a place of duality and intrigue, she thinks, smiling benignly as she looks down the mountain road.

In the middle distance, she can see a black Seat take the corner too fast and hit a wall at speed, sending bricks and stones into the air.

The car continues through the wall, plunging into the gorge below, followed within seconds by an explosion and a ball of flame.

'Awesome', says Dale.

'Sort that one out with GoCar, you miserable bastard', thinks Susan.

GOING UNDERGROUND

I

'Can you help me, please?'

I'm in Bank tube station on my way to work and a woman has just grabbed my arm. She's about my own age and looks confused and a little bit scared. As she moves closer, I can't help noticing that she is not as fragrant as she might be, like she hasn't showered for a while.

Other than that, she looks much like any other commuter. Blue eyes, shortish dark hair, smart clothes. In fact, she looks a little like me: although, just to be clear, I am never less than 100% fragrant.

She is still holding my arm, a little tighter this time. I notice that her breath is a bit stale, too.

'Please. I know this might seem weird, but I'm lost and don't know where...'

I shake her off and walk away, fast, merging into the crowd. It's rush hour and the station is packed, so I lose her quite easily. I'm late for work, but that's just an excuse. The truth is that I just don't want anything to do with her, or with anybody else who tries to talk to me in public.

For some reason, I have always attracted weirdos. Odd people always seem keen to talk with me - from drunks at parties, to nutters on buses. And one thing I've learned is that they are always well worth avoiding.

It's how London works. If we spent all our time talking to strangers, we'd never go anywhere and never get anything done. And we'd be a lot poorer too, as most of them want something, usually my money.

I leave the station and walk to my office, glad to be safely above ground. But I am aware that I will be underground again soon. And I feel a little worried about it, for some reason. I can't get that woman's frightened face out of my mind.

II

Looking back, I can see that I didn't really stand a chance.

I mean, have you ever been to Bank tube station in the rush hour? It's easily the busiest, most congested and most confusing station on the entire underground network, with thousands of passengers changing trains and rushing to work.

Many of them are young and fit, which you need to be to avoid being trampled underfoot. If you suffer from claustrophobia, or are just small and dislike crowds, like me, this is not the place to be at twenty past eight on a Tuesday morning.

In fact, Bank has more passengers than any other tube station - 52 million a year, to be exact. It's an absolute rabbit warren, with 10 platforms, all in different places and at different levels.

This is mainly because it was built under the streets and not under the buildings, as that would have been too difficult and too expensive - there are 31 Grade A listed buildings adjacent to the station.

That's why so many of the tunnels and platforms have sharp curves – it's to avoid minor obstacles like the vaults of the Bank of England – and why you have to 'mind the gap' on the Central Line platforms.

You're probably wondering why I've turned into such a trainspotting anorak. Well, since this 'thing' happened, I've been doing my research.

One thing I've learned is that we trainspotters are usually a romantic lot, in love with the mundane, decrepit and often rather shabby. However, Bank station is an exception – it is not liked or well-spoken of. By anyone.

Here are two of the descriptions of Bank station that I've found:

> 'An evil, twisting, underground spaghetti junction that invites unwitting commuters into its dark tunnels, never to be seen again'.

'A confusing hellhole with one hundred ways to get lost forever.'

If you don't believe me, try Googling it yourself. Here's what you'll find:

'Londoners say Bank Tube Station is the capital's worst' - BBC News.

'The hell that is Bank Station' - Reddit.

Like I say, I didn't really stand a chance. This place was waiting for someone like me.

III

The next morning, as I fought my way off the train, I thought I saw her again. Same coat, same hair, same rather confused facial expression. She was running (as fast as the crowds would allow) up the escalator and, as my route takes me in that direction, I followed. This involved squeezing past women and their handbags, young men and their backpacks and tourists with their suitcases. All annoying at the best of times and even more so today.

At the top, she kept running. I caught glimpses of her moving past the exits, the toilets and the little booth that sells newspapers and sweets. She finally disappeared into a distant part of the station I've never really noticed before. But then, we're all busy with our own lives and tend to notice only what is in front of us at the time and not what might be there, if we bothered to look.

Giving up the chase, I headed for the nearest Costa. It was going to be another long day and the coffee at work is rubbish - we must be the only office in London that still uses those enormous cans of coagulating coffee granules. I won't mention the brand name. As I waited impatiently in the queue, I saw that the route she had taken ran along a deserted and unmarked concourse, leading nowhere in particular.

By now, curiosity had got the better of me, so I decided to have a better look that evening, on my way home - even if meant being late for my beloved son and glass of wine (not necessarily in that order).

Families can be a bind. Mine is not so much a bind as a complex series of arrangements. Arrangements with my ex-husband (my son), my Mother (childcare) and my partner (our new house and his children).

It's called a blended family, apparently, but sometimes being a full-time working mother is not the ideal blend. Are other arrangements available? I wish.

Work was even busier than expected and I was really looking forward to getting home, where that glass of wine I may have mentioned was calling my name. But as I entered the station, I felt compelled to walk back along that same concourse, past the exits, the toilets and the little booth.

No-one else was around and it all seemed a bit sad and unloved, with dirty floors, old newspapers and small piles of rubbish. The concourse seemed to be leading nowhere in particular and I was about to retrace my steps. Then I saw the tunnel.

It was much like any other tunnel on the Underground system: somewhere for passengers to walk, basically - but with no signage or lighting. Rather than being scary, it seemed quite welcoming, with aged yellow bricks around the oval entrance.

I entered and kept walking as it curved gently. Soon, the station behind me was out of sight. In the dim light, I could see advertising posters on the walls: Bovril, Ovaltine, Weetabix. They were a little tatty and out of date, but then, the tunnel probably hadn't been used since the various renovations and upgrades that have taken place over the years, I reasoned.

The tunnel was silent apart from my echoing footsteps. Then, as I walked, I started to hear some noise, quiet at first and growing in volume as I got nearer. The distant rumbling of trains, the footsteps and murmur of people, the smell of cigarettes. And ahead of me, always disappearing from my line of vision, I could see people.

Although they were never quite in full view, I remember them quite clearly: a woman in a tweed coat, a man wearing a hat, another man smoking a pipe, two girls giggling. Next, I heard the station announcements: a rather posh gentleman advising of trains for British Museum, Chancery Lane, Holborn and Post Office.

None of this was surprising at the time. The tunnel obviously led somewhere, even if it was a bit off the beaten track now, probably as the result of station modernisation. I turned back, as I needed to get home to collect my son. Have I mentioned him? Don't worry, I will.

As I left the tunnel and walked towards my platform, I looked back. I couldn't see it, but I knew it was there – dark and slightly mysterious. And I knew I would have to go back there, soon.

IV

The next morning was uneventful, at first. At the office, I mentioned my little adventure to Simon, the guy I work for, over coffee (the horrid office stuff). He was dismissive, as I might have expected.

'So there's a tunnel in the tube station and you can hear trains. And someone who was lost and a bit smelly talked to you. So far, so what. The tube network is full of people and trains. It's what it's for. Unless you think it's ghosts, Hannah,' he sneered, as he walked away.

In fact, ghosts looked like a distinct possibility - if you believe in that sort of thing of course, which I don't. Eating my lunchtime sandwich, I continued my research. I discovered quite a lot, most of it rather scary.

Exhibit one: dead people. The tube system has carved through lots of old cemeteries and plague pits in its time - in fact, there was a large plague pit at Bank. During World War Two, the station was bombed, killing 56 people. And over the years, there have been thousands of suicides across the tube network - around 150 every year.

If you hear a tannoy announcement about a delayed train due to a 'passenger taken unwell', then you'll know that there's been a 'jumper', as they're known. No wonder there's a bucket and spade on every platform. Death and the underground seem to go together rather well. Or do I mean the underworld.

It turns out that a lot of people do believe in ghosts. At Bank, I discover, there have been many reports over the years of strange apparitions and noises - footsteps, doors slamming, children crying, women screaming - and sudden foul, unexplained smells. Just like being at home with my partner, Paul, then. Have I mentioned him? Thought not.

And it's not just smells. One article found that many people have claimed to have been suddenly consumed by an 'overwhelming feeling of desperation and great sadness' when on the underground. But then, who doesn't feel like that on their way to work sometimes?

Having dismissed ghosts and the supernatural, I scoured Google for a more plausible explanation. Construction work, perhaps. CrossRail is one of Europe's biggest construction projects and passes directly beneath Bank, which itself is currently undergoing 600-million pounds-worth of improvements.

So I could have heard building workers, bulldozers, that sort of thing. Which doesn't really help explain the giggling girls or pipe smoking, does it?

Or perhaps I heard a film being made. Apparently, unused parts of the tube network are often used for filming. Transport for London has a whole department dedicated to this and over the years, there have been hundreds of film shoots in the underground. Remember Sliding Doors? Or Skyfall, where Bond had to take a rush-hour train?

That made me feel a lot better. What I heard was probably a film shoot, using a disused part of the station, as this undoubtedly is. A friend of mine once saw Brad Pitt filming in a hotel near where she works, so I was quite keen to see who was in this film shoot. Idris Elba, perhaps?

But then things got a little spooky again.

Remember that station announcement I heard? It turns out that these days, there are no tube stations called Post Office and British Museum. Post Office changed its name to St Pauls in 1937 and British Museum closed in 1933.

So if it isn't a film shoot, set in the 1930s or earlier, it must be ghosts after all. Time to go looking for those cameras. Please let there be cameras.

V

I've started to visit the tunnel more often. Every day, I've ventured a little further and spent a little longer looking around.

At first, I found nothing. No recurrence of what I had heard before and no film set, let alone Idris Elba. There was nothing to see but a long, dark, dusty tunnel.

Then one day, I heard the noises again. Trains rumbling, brakes squealing, station announcements. The echoes of people talking, laughing and coughing. As I walk towards the platform, I start to see them, busily going somewhere, in their raincoats, hats and dresses. They smell a little different, too - perfume, tobacco, body odour and bad breath. It reminded me of visiting elderly relatives when I was young.

I come down here every day now. I don't just hang around the tunnels and platforms - I've started riding the trains and roaming the stations. I prefer visiting the old stations - Buckingham Palace, City Road, Down Street, Essex Road, Mark Lane, Necropolis, St Mary's, Swiss Cottage, Westbourne Park, York Road. These long-closed stations are as real to me as Bank or Oxford Circus are to you.

Sometimes, I leave the stations at street level, and stand on the pavement, watching. I haven't dared talk to anyone yet. I'm not even sure if that is possible - am I part of all this, or just an invisible observer? They say that during the Second World War, Winston Churchill used to go on the

Underground to find out what 'ordinary people' were thinking. Maybe this is all some sort of reality check for me - goodness knows I need one.

I watch people get into cabs, jump on buses, or just hang around in groups, talking, laughing and shouting. A group of men are standing outside a pub, holding pint glasses and telling jokes. Old men are selling newspapers, shouting out the name of their paper. Children cry, young lovers kiss and older couples bicker. Their accents, clothes and hair styles are familiar, but not quite what I am used to: a little like old photographs or films. It's almost like living in black and white, now I think about it.

No-one seems to take any notice of me: in fact, it's almost like I don't exist. People look right through me. Perhaps I am invisible. I never get hungry. And when I get back to Bank, after what seems like a lengthy excursion, no time seems to have elapsed. It's like it never happened, although I know it did. The best thing is that it is all so undemanding. I am a spectator, with no responsibilities - and after my hectic home and work life, that is very welcome. I just watch the world go by, without even knowing what that world is.

The other day, I saw her again, that woman who approached me at Bank station. She saw me looking at her and smiled, almost to herself, before walking away. Since then, it feels like I'm down here all the time. I know I have another life, above ground, and I know that somehow it is going on without me. But I am not dead. This is not a ghost story. Perhaps there are two of me.

I'm not alone, either. Every day I see others like me. I have started to recognise the signs: I know what to look for. There are probably thousands of us. We don't acknowledge each other, we just go about our business on our own, despite not really having any business.

You may have seen us - mostly in your peripheral vision, but sometimes in plain sight. That man striding for a train, but not actually getting on it. The young girl in the queue at Upper Crust, who never buys anything. The older lady in the sensible coat staring at the posters on the tube walls for hours on end. The young guy in the hoodie, waiting for a girlfriend who never arrives. And me, sitting bolt upright in the carriage, looking straight ahead.

We are not entirely happy, I suspect. But we're not unhappy, either. We're a little like extras in a film, always at the margins, never at the centre of the action - except there is no film, there are no cameras.

Some of us are full-time, I reckon. These are rather more dishevelled and confused, but still able to fit in on a crowded train, although there is something about them that does not encourage conversation. Maybe it's the aroma I mentioned earlier. But we rarely talk to strangers on trains anyway, do we. Read your Standard, check your phone, listen to your music, there's nothing to see here.

Others, like me, come and go. Part-timers. Going underground is not what we chose to do, but like many things in life, we fell into it, lured perhaps by the siren call of an unused doorway, a mysterious staircase, wooden escalators strewn with old copies of the Evening News and the butts of untipped cigarettes. Yesterday is all around us and tomorrow never really comes.

After a while, the curiosity dies, replaced by something less positive. I haven't felt that 'overwhelming feeling of desperation and great sadness' yet, but I can sense that it is not too far away. Will I end up as a jumper, perhaps? I don't think so - my life may not be perfect, but it has its moments.

It's a life that I am now only dimly aware of. A job that I love but which is going nowhere, a partner I like but don't love, a son I really love but take for granted, and an elderly, sick mother who is a permanent drain on my emotions.

My life may not be much, but it needs me. I need somehow to find it, but am no longer sure how to do this. To be honest, I'm finding it all a little confusing.

Perhaps I should ask someone. This lady here, rushing to work. She's about my own age, with blue eyes, shortish dark hair, smart clothes. In fact, she looks a little like me. Perhaps even a lot like me. I approach her and grab her arm.

'Can you help me, please?'

She looks at me and her eyes widen a little in surprise. Perhaps she also recognises the similarity. I hold her arm, a little more tightly this time.

'Please. I know this might seem weird, but I'm lost and don't know where...'

She shakes me off and walks away, fast, merging into the crowd. I turn and walk back towards the tunnel, going underground.

GREEN AND PLEASANT LAND
I

The pale sun was casting long thin shadows through the tall trees that lined Big Field, as I parked my car next to the old cricket scoreboard. The air was filled with the smell of fresh grass cuttings and in the distance, I could see rugby posts and a gleaming sports pavilion, its clock showing 11.15. As I had arranged to meet the others at 11.00, I grabbed my jacket and set off hurriedly in what I hoped was the right direction.

'Just keep walking towards the Concert Hall and turn left at the Music Studios, Sir. You'll see the reception committee ahead of you.'

The tall blond youth in whites and a striped blazer pointed me confidently in the right direction and continued his work, organising the car parking with all the effortless authority of an independent school sixth-former.

This place has certainly changed, I thought. If our roles had been reversed, at his age I would have avoided my gaze and mumbled at my shoes, such was my lack of authority and confidence. Yet if he had given me a detention, even now, I would have accepted it.

The sports pavilion has also changed: a major improvement on the dilapidated wooden changing rooms with inadequate sanitation that we used to smoke behind. And who would have imagined that music studios and concert halls would even exist.

But that's the difference between the mediocre state grammar school that I went to all those years ago and the successful independent school it has since become.

Five of us had agreed to meet up at our old school's '500th Anniversary Celebration', an upgraded version of the annual Founder's Day. It was a chance for the school to wallow in its own imagined glory, while recruiting old boys such as us (it was a single-sex school until quite recently) as donors to various bursary schemes, and our children as potential students.

None of us had been active or enthusiastic 'old boys'. I hadn't been back here since I was 18, but, at the instigation of Tubby Akers, we had agreed to give it one last shot. Our plan was to wander around for an hour or so, insult a few of our contemporaries, exchange banter with any members of staff who remembered us, and then then head off for an extended liquid lunch in the town.

The various sporting matches and performances in the afternoon would have to somehow manage without us. And I for one had no intention of signing up as a donor to anything. I'm no socialist, but the idea of subsidising any part of a fee-paying school felt fundamentally wrong.

The Reception Committee - teachers, prefects and admin staff - was disarmingly welcoming and ruthlessly efficient, like an upmarket country house hotel or business-class check-in. I can't remember being treated with such respect once in my entire seven years at School.

Back then, we were repeatedly told how fortunate we were to be at the Grammar School and that, provided we obeyed the rules, a bright future lay ahead. No-one in authority had ever told us we were welcome, smiled at us (unless it preceded some sort of humiliation or punishment) or invited us to have a nice day.

I was pointed in the direction of my group and saw that they were deep in conversation with two attractive young women. For men of our age, the tactic of using attractive female sixth-formers as hosts was inspired, I have to admit. However, I decided to keep an eye on Vince Price, one of our group, a creature of depraved habits even when at school.

After greeting my four colleagues, I met Amy and Izzy, our hosts. Tall, long-haired and supremely self-confident, they were the kind of girl that would once have reduced me to a state of babbling red-faced incoherence.

Now, my hard-earned veneer of sophistication enabled me to deal easily with their relentless enthusiasm, endless hair-flicking and naïve entitlement. And their long legs and short skirts, too.

For Amy and Izzy, the world was all about success, friendships, skiing trips and internships at Daddy's publishing company, before going to the 'Uni' of their choice. They had yet to savour the sour taste of failure and the stale reek of compromise that hung over the five of us old boys – or alumni, as we now seemed to be known.

Anyway, it's time we were all introduced. I mentioned Geoff 'Vincent' Price earlier: known as Vince for short, he is low of brow and evil of intent, and runs an accountancy firm in Redditch. I haven't seen him or Alan 'Chimp' Watson - now partner of a small law firm somewhere in South London - since school.

Vince is still low of brow, but wears 'invisible' hearing aids, while Chimp - named for his hairy body and shambling gait - is now fat and bald. However, the more we spoke, the more the years fell away: the boy inside the man is never far from the surface.

I have been friends with Humph - Quentin Humphries - since we left school. We've met every few years, usually with our families. As with most men who have known each other a long time, we have a checklist of facts about each other - names of wife and children, general nature of job, and so on. But we know almost nothing at all about the inner man.

Despite his posh name, Humph is as rough as they come and was born on a council estate, the son of a large angry man in a vest and his small equally angry wife. Leaving school early at the age of 16, he has made a reasonable stash doing something or other in the 'financial services' industry and is now semi-retired, sitting on the board of various small local companies.

He is still a rough diamond, but a well-groomed one, looking cool - much as I hate to admit it - in expensive clothes, Rolex watch and a permanent tan. He was - and is - a ladies man and we used to joke that he left school with more children than O levels to his name.

And then there's me - Robin Boyce. Rob to my friends, but known at school as Boy Wonder, or Blunder for short.

Unlike the Robin who was Batman's sidekick, I am tall, dark and (so I am told) handsome. I can't remember who told me that, since you ask, and it was probably quite a few years ago. But I've aged reasonably well, anyway.

After a patchy career in the lower reaches of the entertainment industry, in the 90s I set up my own recording studio business with a similarly disillusioned colleague, doing voice-overs for ads and videos, and making programmes for in-flight entertainment. We sold out a few years ago - not for a fortune, but just about enough to save me from bankruptcy following my divorce.

The fifth and final member of our group was Nicholas 'Tubby' Akers, without whom none of us would be here today. I'm not sure that any of us had been in contact with him since school, but the internet is a powerful tool and he had managed to track us all down. It's not as though we were hard to find: the needy ones on LinkedIn, the successful via Google and the saddest on Facebook, sharing photographs of their holidays and family.

Akers came across as a jovial character - a little plump and shiny perhaps, as his name suggests - who subtly exhibited all the trappings of success. He's something to do with hedge funds and is absolutely minted, apparently. Humph told me that he saw him arrive in a Ferrari - one of the rare ones. He now calls himself Nick, but that is going to be a hard one - he was always known as Tubby at school, a name given to him by the head sports master, Dicky Dawson. And Tubby he still is.

'It's fantastic to see all you guys again,' said Tubby. 'I'm really looking forward to finding out what you've all been up to since school.'

Before we could confirm his suspicions - probably, his knowledge - that compared to him, we are all provincial mediocrities, the tones of the Headmaster boomed fruitily through the PA system. He's not the Headmaster from our era, obviously - Henshaw was a doddering, incompetent old fool who is long dead. I realise with a start that he was probably younger then than I am now.

By contrast, the new Head, Charles Smith, is young - mid-40s - and dynamic. He is taking the school places and is undoubtedly destined for greater things.

His speech said all that you might expect, but in a way that - despite ourselves - we found uplifting and even moving. By the time it came to singing the school song – Jerusalem, as you might have expected – the five of us had our arms around each other's shoulders and were bellowing out the song with tears in our eyes. If he could do this to hardboiled cynics like us, what must he do to his students? Despite ourselves, we were impressed.

'Whatever we might think of the school, this really is England's green and pleasant land, isn't it,' I said to the others, looking around me. 'Perhaps there is a God after all.'

'There is indeed a God, Blunder,' said Humph, smirking and gesturing with his head towards the stage, where we see an emaciated Dicky Dawson, our former sports master, in a baggy Loughborough College Blazer and a wheelchair. Presumably suffering from something terminal, he was a shadow of the terrifying figure he once was.

'It couldn't have happened to a nicer man,' said Tubby, speaking for us all - Dawson was much disliked. 'Shall we go for a stroll?'

We said goodbye to Amy and Izzy, who express almost genuine disappointment at not being able to join us in the pub later, and set off on our stroll.

II

There was little that we recognised, as we shambled past an impressive laboratory block that NASA would be proud of. Most of the school had changed for the better – not that difficult, it's true. The old wartime huts - of which there were many - had all been replaced by new buildings and most of the shabby old school buildings had been refurbished or rebuilt.

Lying at the heart of it all, the small building that had some claim to being 500 years old, like the school, had been painted white and re-named The Rudkin Centre, presumably after some generous millionaire old boy.

The pupils - or students, as they are now called - had changed most of all. The ones we pass are all disarmingly friendly, happy and well-adjusted, almost as if they enjoy being here. It took me years after leaving school to achieve that level of maturity. If only I could turn back time and do it all again, I thought.

'So what on earth possessed you to come back to school, Tubby?' said Vince. 'None of the rest of us were exactly high achievers, but I can't imagine you have that many happy memories, what with the bullying and so on. Not that I had anything to do with that, as I hope you know.'

'That's a fair point, Vince,' says Tubby. 'And no, I don't hold any grudges against any of you guys. Even you, Blunder.'

I'm not sure why he mentioned me. What had I done? Tubby went on to provide some reassurance.

'It really wasn't as bad for me as you might think. After all, the school got me through enough exams for Cambridge. And as a result of that maths degree - a double first, if I could be allowed to boast - I did pretty well for myself in the city, got married, all the usual stuff.'

'Let's be honest, Tubby,' says Chimp. 'You must have made a shitload of money from that hedge fund of yours. I saw the car you rolled up in - and I bet that's not the only one you've got.'

'Well if you really want to know, Chimp old chap, yes, I've got quite a collection of vintage cars at home. Some of them are worth a fair bit, like the one I brought today. And yes, I have indeed made a shitload of money. But I'll be blowed if the school is going to get any of it, no matter what those two girls offer me.'

We all cheered - both at his refusal to subsidise the school and at the opportunity to make various lewd suggestions regarding Amy, Izzy and Akers comment about being blowed. Clearly, our attitudes to women are rooted in the past and getting together has brought out the worst in us. More surprisingly, we all seemed to resent the school in some way, possibly because most of the bullying and so on was led by the staff rather than the pupils.

Dickie Dawson, the sports master, was probably the worst offender. He knew that Akers - short, fat and half-blind, peering anxiously through his NHS round spectacles - was never going to be a rugby player. Despite this, he used Akers as a sort of human punch bag, to teach the rest of us how to tackle.

This was one of many small humiliations inflicted on Akers over the years. Despite this, he seemed to be seeking reconciliation, not revenge, and was probably the most open and enthusiastic of us all. While he was talking with the others about his car collection, which didn't particularly interest me, I fell a little behind the group, checking my phone.

I looked up to see two masters from our era walking by: Guts and Socks. George Guthrie – aka Guts - was a former Army Officer who had taught geography and was Head of Sixth Form. He and Socks - his close friend, Cyril Beddows, who taught German - were two of the few masters we had all liked and respected.

Guts and Socks were from the wartime generation. Incredibly strict when on duty and in their classroom, they were relaxed and laissez-faire when off duty. I was somehow extremely pleased to see them.

Guts waved his umbrella at me genially. 'Good morning Boyce, my dear boy. What a lovely day for the Headmaster's little event. However, Mr Beddows and I have been unable to resist the siren call of the White Hart, so we're adjourning there now for a richly-deserved drink or two.'

I recalled that the two of them were also piss-artists, who never missed the opportunity for a drink, richly-deserved or not.

'This means that regretfully we're going to miss the rest of today's fun,' continued Guts, smiling in a way that suggested the opposite.

'But I'm sure we'll hear all about it in due course. Should you and your young friends decide to go to the pub later, it would be gratefully appreciated if you could avoid the saloon bar. We'd hate to have to report you to our brilliant young Headmaster, or anything like that, my dear old chap.'

'Thank you for the advice, Sir,' I replied. 'We'll be sure not to bump into you.'

'Good man, Boyce,' said Guts, baring his teeth in a rictus grin that drew attention to the broken red veins on his face and the yellowing moustache. Bidding me farewell, they strode in a military manner towards the corner of the gardens, leaving an aroma of pipe tobacco hanging in the air.

I re-joined the rest of the group, who were still discussing cars. Apparently, Vince and Chimp both keep old sports cars in the garages of their executive homes - an MG and a Mazda respectively - that they wheel out at weekends. They seemed unable to recognise the disparity between their low-budget suburban hobby and Akers rare and valuable collection.

I decided to interrupt. 'Did you see old Guts and Socks back there? They haven't changed a bit, have they. Still smoking pipes and going to the pub, the drunken old gits.'

None of the others had seen them and furthermore, there was some surprise at my announcement.

'What do you mean, they haven't changed a bit?' said Chimp. 'They must have been dead for years Blunder, you silly sod.'

'Yes, just think about it,' added Humph. 'Guts retired when we were in the Lower Sixth - so he'd be more than 100 years old by now. And Socks can't be that much younger. Are you sure it was them?'

'Of course it was them. They were both smoking pipes and heading to the pub, like they always do. We had a chat and Guts advised me which bar they'd be in, as usual. Who else could it have been?'

I realised that the others were right and felt a little confused. I was sure it was Guts and Socks - but how could it have been? And why would they worry about having to report me - I am fairly obviously a grown man, not a sixth-former. Before I could think about it any further, there was a shout from Akers.

'Hey guys - look what I've found.'

Akers was at the end of a passageway, by an old wall. He was kneeling by a trapdoor, half-hidden by weeds and uncut grass, which he was trying to open.

'Bloody hell,' said Vince. 'It must be Plotter's Caves.'

The site of many an illicit cigarette when we were at school - Number 6 and Embassy were the brands of choice - Plotter's Caves were enshrined in local history as the location for the Gunpower Plot conspirators, as well as the site of the CCF shooting range.

The main entrance was under lock and key in the Headmaster's Gardens, but there had been various 'secret' entrances around the school grounds - long since sealed-off - sometimes involving perilous climbs down into the caves via the wooden scaffolding that stopped it all from collapsing.

We all helped Akers pull at the trapdoor until it opened. We filed in and walked down the narrow passageway to a larger area, where the passage had been widened to create a room.

Behind us, there was a loud bang as the doors slammed shut. We rushed back, to find that the doors were clearly locked from the outside.

In the dim light, we could see that there were now only four of us in the cave.

III

Akers strolled along the footpath towards the Teaching Block, his hands in his pockets and a big smile on his face.

That was just too good an opportunity to miss – how could he not have slammed that trapdoor shut? He'd walk around the block for ten minutes and then go back to let the guys out.

As he turned the corner, he reached a part of the school he didn't remember. A number of dilapidated classroom buildings, looking like wartime relics, lay either side of the path. As he passed one, an angry red-faced school master, in a chalk-encrusted black gown, shouted at him from the doorway.

'You boy. Yes, you. What on earth do you think you're doing wandering around as though you own the place? You're late, come in and join the rest of the class immediately. And get your hands out of your pockets immediately, you're not here to enjoy yourself.'

At one time, Akers would have obeyed, instinctively. But he is no longer young and fat, he is simply plump and prosperous - a successful and supremely confident businessman. He knows exactly how to deal with this and assumes the arrogant form of politeness much loved in the City.

'My dear chap, I think you must be mistaken. You see, I'm...'

'How dare you, boy,' explodes the Master, his face reddening.

'*You* think *I'm* mistaken? You absurd little worm. There's only one person here who is mistaken and he is short, fat and standing right in front of me, wearing silly little round glasses. Now get in that classroom immediately before I reach for my trusted friend, Mr Whippy.'

By now, faces are pressed against the windows, enjoying the diversion. This is far better than one of Old Stewpot's history lessons and they are keen for it to continue for as long as possible.

'Get back to your desks immediately, or it will be Saturday mornings for the lot of you.'

Defeated, Akers walked into the classroom. This is probably something organised by the school as part of the event, he thought. A roleplay exercise by the drama society, perhaps. It could be entertaining and he can always leave at any time. This man is obviously in character and it would be churlish of Akers not to play along.

He found an empty desk and sat down. The rest of the class were boys, around the age of 14 or 15. They no longer seemed interested in him and were reluctantly turning towards the front, shuffling books, pens and papers.

'Right, where were we before I was so rudely interrupted?' said Old Stewpot, vigorously cleaning the blackboard.

'The American War of Independence, Sir,' said a tousle-haired boy seated at the front, to boos, hisses and whispers of 'creep'.

'Yes indeed, the American War of Independence. Well done, Jones. Now then, it is commonly assumed that the American forces were massively superior, in terms of both strategy and resources, which is why the British surrendered. However, the situation was far more complex than that, as you will know from reading the chapter in the set book that I gave you to read last week. Why was it far more complex, Lander?'

Lander, who was slumped at his desk near the back, staring out of the window, did not answer. He was either asleep or in some sort of stupor, which is why he had been selected for the question.

He was soon wide awake again, knocked backwards by the force of the blackboard duster, thrown at his head with great power and accuracy. A skill you just don't see these days, thinks Akers. Lander looked around him, surrounded by a cloud of white dust, confused and in some pain.

'You were saying, Lander?'

'I'm sorry sir, could you repeat the question please sir?'

'No sir, I cannot repeat the question. Now, I'm disappointed Gentlemen. Extremely disappointed. This is not the standard of intellectual cut and thrust I was promised when I joined the elite teaching staff of this fine school. I was promised bright young men, eager to drink at the fountain of knowledge, ready to learn, analyse and debate. You are a big disappointment, Lander. Join me and my trusty flexible friend afterwards, and together we will discover a new and altogether more painful type of cut and thrust. Anyone else?'

Jones was straight in, with a detailed answer to the question. Akers realised with a start that he needed to get back to the cave to let the others out. He stood and walked towards the door.

'Thank you for a most entertaining lesson, Mr - Stewart, is it? That really did bring back some memories, but I'm afraid I have to leave now.'

'Most entertaining? How dare you, boy.'

Stewart was, again, furious. 'You think you are sufficiently qualified to comment on my lesson – me, a graduate of the great University of Oxford and you, an overweight, spotty, masturbatory fourth-former. Of course you can't leave. Sit down immediately and don't say another word until the end of the lesson - unless you wish to join our unfortunate friend Lander later for a taste of Mr Whippy. Is that clear?'

'Well, Mr Stewart, I'm sorry, but I really do have to...'

'I said 'is that clear', boy. It was rhetorical and I did not expect an answer. Do you know what rhetorical means?'

'It comes from the Greek, sir, meaning a question designed not to elicit information but to produce an effect or make a point.'

Old Stewpot is momentarily silenced and seems inordinately pleased at this response.

'Well done, boy - Akers, isn't it. Despite myself, I'm impressed. Maybe you're not such an imbecile after all. Now, sit down and you may leave at the end of the lesson, like everyone else. Except Lander, of course.'

The lesson continues without incident. As the bell signifying the end of the lesson goes, Stewart holds up his hands, preventing anyone from moving.

'Do not leave just yet - I have an announcement to make. Mr Dawson, our beloved sports master, he of the red nylon tracksuit and whistle, has asked me to let this class know that no fewer than seven of you have been selected for the Under-15s team for Saturday's game against Tonbridge. This is a record number for a single class, apparently, so well done to Brown, Daniels, Grey, Harris, Kinloch, Pollard and - his first selection for the A team - Akers.'

The class cheers and Akers is slapped on the back several times.

'Well done Akers, they won't find a way past you.'

'See you at lunch, Nick. You need feeding up, big man.'

Lunch! Akers remembers that it's sausages today - his favourite. There's something about a school sausage. He walks towards the dining room, chatting with his new classmates. One of them has the new Pink Floyd album under his arm, which they are discussing.

After lunch, which he spends with his new team-mates, it's maths, his favourite subject. He quickly masters quadratic equations and is asked to demonstrate his skills on the blackboard. To overcome the jeers and cries of 'creep' from the rest of the class, he draws a cock and balls on the board while the master is facing the class, wiping it out before returning to his desk amidst cheers.

It turns out that Tubby Akers is popular with his classmates, top of the class at most subjects and good at games. Who knew?

IV

In Plotter's Caves, our tempers were getting a little frayed. We had tried to break down the trap door, with no success - it was made of solid wood, locked and, as it was horizontal, too heavy to lift - and there was only room for one of us to stand underneath it at a time. The tunnel was boarded-up, making walking further into the caves impossible.

Shouting got no response - we were in a remote part of the grounds, we remembered. While we had mobiles, the only person nearby that we could call was Akers - and he wasn't answering. There were always the emergency services, but we thought we'd leave that embarrassment for a little longer. We agreed that we would sit it out - Akers would return soon, the joke would be over and we could then head to the pub, with the drinks on him.

So we sat tight and talked. The first hour or so had been bearable. We had traded jokes and stories about our days at school, talked about our lives since then and discussed our reactions to the day's events. I had again raised my strange sighting of Guts and Socks, which none of them was prepared to take seriously.

Then, someone farted. It was greeted with the usual reaction. First, the disdainful cries and shouts, demanding to know who was responsible and calling whoever it was the dirty bastard that he was. This was closely followed by the second stage - genuine shock and disgust as the vile fumes spread and entered our nostrils, accompanied by exaggerated fanning of the air, coughing, and pantomime choking, gagging and holding of the throat.

It was at this point that the perpetrator would usually give himself up, by laughing proudly or making a humorous remark.

But no-one did. We all swore in turn that it wasn't one of ours - even Humph, who boasted that we'd soon have known if it was one of his.

'Maybe it was Guts or Socks,' suggested Chimp. 'The fart from beyond the grave.'

That was when we decided that we really did want to leave. We were hungry and thirsty, we were uncomfortable and at least two of us were bursting for a pee, one of us for something much worse. And on top of that, we were now sharing a confined space with a paranormal flatulator.

Akers was getting less popular by the minute and we started to discuss what we'd do to him when he returned. This led us to discuss what had been done to him in the past.

'Do you remember the rugby?' asked Vincent. 'That bastard Dawson really made him suffer with all that tackling crap.'

I can see us all now, lined up in our rugby kit on the school playing field. 'Start running, Tubby,' Dawson would say, giving Akers ten seconds to waddle up the pitch, before blowing his whistle. One at a time, we'd chase after Akers and dive into him at high speed, wrapping our arms around his chubby legs and bringing him down in a red-faced, muddy heap.

Rising to our feet, we'd leave him to pick himself up and walk sadly back, blinking and breathless, to his starting position, ready for the next tackler. He seemed to accept it as his lot in life, but none of us could meet his eye.

'And what about the camping trips in the Brecon Beacons?' said Humph. 'God knows what happened to him, but whatever it was, it wasn't nice.'

There were two masters who spent much of their spare time organising all manner of extra-curricular activities: canoeing, foreign trips, Duke of Edinburgh Awards and Scouts were just some of them.

Their effort and commitment could not be doubted and they were responsible for countless acts of genuine kindness and generosity. Many boys gained experiences they would not otherwise have had and some received support they just wouldn't have found elsewhere.

However, there was a dark side and not for nothing were the masters in question known as 'Pervy' Peters and 'Dodgy' Davidson.

Peters, who taught modern languages, was a large, dishevelled man in his late thirties, with short hair and a craggy, lined face. He spoke with a slight South London edge to his voice and invariably wore baggy grey trousers and a badly-ironed blue shirt.

Davidson, who taught Chemistry, was a little older - maybe in his early forties. He was short, dark and smarter, better-spoken and better-groomed than Peters. Both were unmarried and continued to live close to the school until long past their retirement, eating lunch in the dining room every day and attending school functions.

On the camping trip in question, Pervy had been leading the way as we ascended the mountain, hiking up a grassy footpath. The area was deserted and the sun was shining. Halfway up, Pervy stripped off all his clothes and led the way, stark naked apart from his rucksack, singing opera at the top of his voice. No-one said a thing.

We pitched our tents and, as the temperature dropped, climbed into our sleeping bags. Tubby made the mistake of saying loudly that he was freezing cold. He was ordered to enter the tent occupied by Peters and Davidson, which was pitched away from the rest of us, so that he could be warmed-up.

Tubby 'was very quiet the next morning and we never asked what happened. We simply packed-up and walked back down the mountain.

Talking about this forty years later, trapped in a cave, led us to share more experiences, stories and rumours of a similar nature. There were quite a few - none of them damning in their own right, but all involving the same names and suggestive of - at best - a culture of men and boys in close proximity, often without clothes. At worst - well, we had no evidence of that, but the circumstantial evidence kept on coming.

Our conversation also led to the realisation that two of the Head Boys from our era - Simpson and Cooper - had later been imprisoned for sexual offences against young men. Until then, just two of us had known about Simpson, and only one about Cooper.

Inevitably perhaps, both had been keen supporters of extracurricular activities and were close to Peters and Davidson. The four of us now suspected that something rather unpleasant had been taking place under our noses and were struggling to come to terms with our ignorance and naivety. Or perhaps we just hadn't wanted to know.

'What a school,' said Vince. 'All that going on and it's taken us until now to put it all together. It makes me sick to think how stupid we were not to notice - let alone our failure to say or do anything about it. And there they all are, making speeches, celebrating what a great place this is and singing hymns. I bet that new Headmaster doesn't know the half of it.'

'England's green and pleasant land, my arse,' agreed Chimp.

V

It all happened quickly. The trapdoor was suddenly flung open and we had to shield our eyes against the light. We could just about make out two men looking down at us, silhouetted against the sun

'Well, well, well. Look what we've got here,' said the first figure, a large man in his late thirties. 'Humphries, Price, Boyce and Watson. A right little group of skivers. What on earth do you four think you're doing down here, when you should be on the School Run with everyone else?'

'I'd say they'd been smoking, wouldn't you?' said the second figure, a smaller man in his forties. 'Alright you horrible little lot, let's see you get out of that cave and then you can turn out your pockets.'

Humph was not happy. 'Who the hell are they? If they think they can talk to us like that, they can think again.'

'Too right,' added Chimp, 'Let's get up there and sort them out.'

We climbed out of the caves and stood in a semi-circle around the two men, who seemed somehow older and larger than us. They were clearly schoolmasters and were strangely familiar, but I couldn't put a name to their faces.

71

Things were about to kick-off - Chimp and Humph in particular were looking aggressive - when we were interrupted by Guts and Socks, weaving their way back from the White Hart.

'Good afternoon, Mr Peters and Mr Davidson,' hailed a slurred voice. 'A lovely afternoon for it, isn't it.'

'Hello there, Mr Guthrie,' said Peters. 'We just found these reprobates lurking in the caves, smoking and goodness knows what else. Mr Davidson and I were about to discuss what punishment to mete out.'

'We'll leave that in your capable hands,' said Guthrie. 'Just don't be too lenient, that's all I ask. These boys have to be taught a lesson, the more vicious and unfair the better. They'll thank you for it when they're grown-up, you mark my words.' With that, Guthrie and Beddows stumbled off.

'What the hell is going on,' whispered Humph. 'Guts and Socks should be dead, Pervy and Dodgy must be in their 80s and the four of us are all adults. Yet here they are. And here we are.'

'Now listen, I don't know who you two are exactly, but there seems to be some sort of mistake,' began Vince. 'We're old boys of the school, here to attend the 500th anniversary celebrations. If you could just point us in the direction of the main school buildings, we'll be on our way.'

'And may I remind you that we take your threat of punishment extremely seriously,' added Chimp. 'We reserve all our rights in this matter and won't hesitate to take legal action against you and the school if necessary.' He was a solicitor, after all.

'Very good boys,' said Pervy, smiling menacingly. 'Now let me tell you what's going to happen. It would be a great shame for you if the Head were to hear of this, so let's keep it all between the six of us. Fortunately, the rest of the school is on the annual School Run at the moment - they'll all be miles away over on the Heath by now. So we are going to walk to the Changing Rooms over there, where the four of you will strip off and bend over.'

He paused, while a strange smirk played across his face. 'Mr Davidson and I will then administer punishment, probably of a rather cruel and unusual kind.'

'Then you can lick your wounds, put on your running vests and join the tail-end of the run,' added Davidson. 'No one need ever know what's happened and your school records will remain unblemished. Unlike your backsides.'

With Davidson and Peters leading the way, the four of us walked towards the changing room. We had accepted our fate. Perhaps it's what we deserved, for looking the other way too many times.

In the distance, we saw Akers, fresh-faced and wearing school uniform, walking to his car. He had one arm around Amy, the taller and more attractive of our sixth-form hosts. She turned, smiled and waved at us.

LONG DRIVE SOUTH

I

'Highway to hell. I'm on the highway to hell.'

Paul Johnson has got the music up loud and is singing along with AC/DC, car window open. He's heading south, driving at 85 mph in the fast lane of the MI.

It's freezing cold outside and the rain is turning to sleet, making his face cold and wet. But when you're driving with a hangover, a really bad hangover at that, you need all the help you can get.

Everyone one has a favourite band, one that stays with them all their lives, like a football team. AC/DC are Paul's. The band was formed more than 40 years, before Paul was even born, but his uncle and elder brother loved them, so he's grown up listening to them: it's a family tradition. His friends tease him about his unfashionable and unsophisticated heavy rock tastes, but he isn't going to change now.

In a way, today is a rare treat. He rarely gets to play AC/DC much these days, and certainly not at this volume, what with the wife and baby. Luckily, his car has a CD player - one of an increasingly small number of cars that does - and his entire collection of the band's CDs is stashed in the glove box and door pockets. Old friends, ready and waiting.

He turns the volume down a little: heavy rock and hangovers need careful handling. And this hangover - the inevitable result of what Paul and his mates would once have called a 'big night' - needs kid gloves.

Not many mates or big nights now, he thinks. Like heavy rock, they're not compatible with a family. It's probably just as well - he's not sure he could take too many hangovers like this one anymore.

Last night had involved some serious drinking with the marketing team from his major client, EuroCom, followed by a few hours sleep in a Leeds Travelodge. Paul works for RLA, a specialist marketing technology company, and EuroCom is one of their biggest clients.

The work isn't glamorous or creative, but there's a lot of it. The margins were slim, but the volume ensured it was a profitable account, one that would interest businesses a lot bigger than RLA.

After a big greasy breakfast, and a steady intake of Red Bull and paracetamol, his headache had subsided to a steady throb. Thus refreshed, he'd started his drive home at about midday - a little later than planned, but with a following wind, he'd still make it back to Sussex in time for dinner. As long as he takes it easy, he should be fine, he reasons.

This will be the first Christmas that Paul and Sarah, his wife, will spend as a family with their son, Nathan, who was born in May. He's definitely his father's son, with a permanent thirst, prodigious nappy-filling capabilities, and a scream to rival that of Brian Johnson, the lead singer of AC/DC. Fortunately, Nathan lacks Brian's Geordie accent: it's bad enough being woken up at 4.00 in the morning, without having to endure that as well, thinks Paul.

Last night had been a big mistake, he reflects.

If he hadn't drunk so much, he wouldn't be feeling so dreadful now. And he certainly wouldn't have slept with his assistant, Laura. However, he can't help feeling impressed that, despite the alcohol, he'd somehow managed to meet her exacting requirements. Or did he, he can't really remember. Either way, she was now on the train back to her parents in Stirling, thank God, so with any luck it would all be forgotten by the New Year.

He takes a swill of Red Bull and carries on singing along with AC/DC. Something about a one-way ride.

II

Fifty miles further south, it's still freezing cold and the sleet has turned to snow, causing Paul to close the car window and turn up the heating. The windscreen wipers are fighting a losing battle, but he keeps up his speed in the fast lane. The phone rings. Just what he needed – Clive Ryder, his boss.

A failed Shakespearean actor, Clive Ryder has achieved much of his business success by the expert utilisation of a single tactic: shouting at people until they agree with him. It is not taught at business schools but is surprisingly effective.

Ryder is the only man Paul has ever known who literally froths at the mouth when speaking (or rather, shouting. He never speaks). The consequences of this when being shouted at by him in person are not worth contemplating. His voice over the car speakers is as loud as the rock music it replaces.

'Paul', he bellows festively. 'How are you? And how's your lovely wife, err, Susan. Sorry, Sarah. And the little one, Natalie. Ah, Nathan, of course. Anyway, I was just calling to wish you all a very Happy Christmas'.

Ryder was a man for whom small talk held about as much interest as foreplay does to a dog. A quick sniff and on with the main event, thinks Paul.

'So how was the trip?' shouts Ryder. 'Did you get the contract signed?'

He lets the sentence hang in the air. The contract: the main purpose of Paul's trip to Leeds. His main task for the past three months had been to finalise RLA's contract with EuroCom for next year. He had consistently failed to raise the issue with the most senior client contact, Trevor Helliwell, and had hoped to rectify this by discussing it in person with him last night.

They'd have had a quiet conversation over a drink, man to man, Helliwell nodding and smiling in agreement with some of Paul's wise words. He'd have readily agreed to sign the contract the following day. Hands would have been shaken and backs slapped.

Instead, there had been a brief conversation outside the meeting room, Helliwell leaving for home immediately after the meeting, his farewell cursory at best. Paul had been left with the more junior members of the team, keen drinkers to a man (and woman), but not decision-makers.

Ryder wasn't giving up. 'Paul, please let me know you've got it signed. It will be out of my hands if this doesn't come off - as you know, the board are keen to cut costs and I can't justify employing a guy like you without a major contract such as EuroCom.'

Ryder was warming to his task and Paul could picture the spittle turning to foam on either side of his mouth. His voice was increasing in volume and Paul could see why people agreed with him so readily, rather than try to battle his relentless, saliva-fuelled, onslaught.

'Paul, listen to me. You're not a young man of promise anymore. You've got responsibilities now and I'd hate to see a great guy like you out on the street. Not that we want to lose you, obviously, but…'

Paul decided to improvise, hoping that a few well-chosen lies would buy him some time.

'Look Clive, the meeting could not have gone better. We went out for a quiet meal and Trevor was as good as gold all evening. He loves what we do and I'm confident he'll be signing off the contract very soon, now that things have quietened down a bit. You know how busy they are at this time of year up there.'

'This can't wait any longer, Paul. Why not call him now to check and get back to me immediately. We just can't afford to leave this until next year. If you don't speak to him, I will.'

As Ryder rang off, Paul could hear him yelling something to his long-suffering secretary, Yvonne. Did he ever speak normally? Did he shout sweet nothings to his wife at bedtime? Paul shuddered as he briefly contemplated a vision of Ryder, raving and frothing at the mouth, mounting poor Mrs Ryder.

The phone call to Helliwell can wait, he thinks, as he reaches for the Red Bull, turns the music up and resumes singing.

The motorway stretches into the distance, illuminated by the dim red lights of other vehicles, barely visible through the falling snow. Brian Johnson is singing about how he is never going to die.

III

On the other side of the M1, Quarter-Pounder and Spike are heading back to base at speed. As he eases the BMW beyond 80, Spike turns to his partner.

'Thank God there was nothing too serious today - looks like we'll be back in good time to really savour that first pint. Especially as that bastard Jacko is paying.'

PCs Mick 'Spike' Milligan and Ben 'Quarter-Pounder' McDonald are heading back to base in Nottingham after a long shift patrolling the motorway. So far, their customers have included: a minibus full of friendly Muslims, pulled up on the hard shoulder for prayers; a battered Peugeot 205 reeking of cannabis fumes, driven by an abusive young man, egged on by his tracksuit-wearing mates; and a Romanian lorry driver, caught on camera throwing a fresh two-litre bottle of steaming urine from his cab.

No deaths or injuries fortunately - although they've both seen their fair share of those. They'd laugh it off with their mates in the pub, but for weeks afterwards they'd lie awake at night, unable to forget what they'd seen. Spike thought of one such case a few months ago, involving a mother and her children.

'Now that trucker really was taking the piss,' says Quarter-Pounder, lightening the mood. 'As if our job's not tough enough already.'

Large and shaven-headed, he doesn't say much, preferring to grunt whenever possible. Like Spike, he enjoys the banter and harbours a secret ambition to appear on one of the many television programmes about the Police. Police Interceptors, say, or Traffic Cops. His preference would be Police UK: Armed and Deadly, but fortunately for everyone, Quarter-Pounder and Spike don't carry guns.

In the meantime, there's the Christmas Piss-Up to contend with. Their division of the Nottinghamshire Special Operations Unit is meeting this evening, starting in town at their favourite Wetherspoons, The Friar Tuck. From there, who knows - but it wouldn't be pretty. Their sergeant - Paul 'Jacko' Jackson - is buying the first round, which no-one wants to miss.

'And as for those young guys smoking dope,' continues Quarter-Pounder, 'it's all very well patting the little shits on the head and giving them a warning, but we both know what can happen with drivers under the influence.'

'Don't worry about it mate, we'll soon be off shift and on the lash,' replies Spike, overtaking a long line of traffic. 'As long as none of the muppets out there does anything stupid in the next half-hour, that is.'

IV

Paul is driving smoothly through the darkness, heating cranked up, music playing, wipers on. A traffic report interrupts the music, rousing him from that deep state of semi-consciousness known only to drivers, whereby you have absolutely no idea where you are and hope to God you haven't been asleep.

The traffic report mostly states the obvious: road and weather conditions are terrible, heavy traffic and driving snow can be expected, motorists are urged to take care. More importantly, there are long delays on the motorway twenty miles further south, with two lanes closed, because of a broken-down lorry.

To make matters worse, the heavy snow will be accompanied by freezing fog in the Sherwood Radio area, says Julie, the traffic reporter. She hands over to a cheesy DJ called Robbie Kempton.

'Thanks Julie, me old mate. So remember friends, if you're driving home for Christmas, make sure you've got snow tyres on your sledge. And here's Chris Rea'.

Buggeration, thinks Paul. Better call the wife. It looks like he'll be late after all, flowers and cap in hand. After a few false starts, he manages to use the voice control and is speaking to Sarah.

'Hello darling, how have you and Johnson Junior been coping? Has he? Good...Yes, I'm well on the way. It's busy and there are a few delays....yes, snow and so on... but I'll be back as soon as I can...before eight for sure...Yes the meeting went well - another big client in the bag, courtesy of the old PJ magic...Oh just a few drinks, a quick curry and an early night...Laura? Oh, she took her fat backside home to Scotland straight after the meeting, leaving me to hold the fort, as usual. That girl is such a pain...No, I only had a few, like I said...Yes, of course I'm fine to drive... A few hours...look, I don't do this for fun you know."

Why am I always the bad guy, thinks Paul.

"Yes, I know you've got a lot to cope with...Yes, I know there's 12 of us for Christmas lunch and...so have I and...No, I haven't asked Clive for a pay rise yet...yes, I know you want new furniture...yes, I know...yes...yes...yes, a takeaway will be fine...OK see you later.'

Paul thumps the steering wheel angrily and reaches for another can of Red Bull. Stifling a yawn, he turns the music up and opens the window. The 150 miles still ahead of him seem more daunting than he first thought, but he presses on. His mind goes back into neutral and he relives some of the past 24 hours.

The brief meeting in the corridor with Trevor Helliwell hadn't gone as well as he would have liked and nowhere near as well as he had told Ryder. Helliwell had been striding down the corridor, with Paul in pursuit.

'Quite honestly Paul, I'm not sure I'll be able to sign this contract.' Helliwell had said, pulling on his coat and not even bothering to look back over his shoulder at Paul.

'There have been one or two issues this year, as you know, and the team think there are other people out there that may be better suited to our needs. I'll be in touch.'

Why couldn't I have come back with something more powerful than just nodding and saying that I quite understood, thinks Paul. They need us and Helliwell ought to know that, rather than giving me all that 'my team' nonsense. Team? What do that bunch of morons know, with their degrees from third-rate universities and about three years experience between the lot of them? Let's work as a team and do things my way, that's how Paul would run that department.

And then there's Laura. Laura, of all people. He doesn't even like her, certainly doesn't find her attractive and thought that this was mutual. They worked together well and there had been absolutely no chemistry, no frisson, not even a hint. But after a few drinks she was all over him and he hadn't been able to resist.

Why hadn't he just gone to his room and got a decent night's sleep? God knows he could have done with it: if he wasn't driving, he could drop off to sleep at any minute, given the chance.

Paul is a simple, well-meaning, man, but weak. He loves his wife to heaven and back. He wants to be loyal, to be a good provider, to be a good husband and father - not some drunken womaniser.

He vows to turn over a new leaf and his mind drifts away, thinking of what he needs to do to achieve this. It's all about empathy, he decides - be there for Sarah, understand her problems and needs, help her when you can, learn how to change nappies.

Lost in a world of stinking nappies, he rapidly returns to full consciousness. The traffic in the two inside lanes has slowed down, as Paul approaches the lane closures. He knows exactly how to deal with this sort of thing: be aggressive, be positive and don't slow down until you absolutely have to.

And most importantly, don't under any circumstances move into an inside lane too early and get stuck there like an idiot - leave it to the absolute last minute.

Keeping his speed up, he stays in the outside lane, overtaking miles of crawling traffic. At the last minute, as planned, he pulls across sharply into the middle lane, much to the annoyance of a van driver, who flashes his lights.

He then cuts in front of an Audi in the inside lane, braking hard as he tucks in behind a lorry, swerving to a rapid halt, wheels screaming in protest.

That certainly woke me up, thinks Paul. A few gestures and angry faces to ignore, too. But just as quickly as it had developed, the congestion starts to clear and he is able to drive away, accelerating smoothly into the clear road ahead.

He looks at the blue skies breaking through the clouds and smiles. Nothing to it, he thinks.

V

Gradually, the drive becomes more pleasant. Much more pleasant: there is less traffic and the weather starts to improve. I might make it back home in time after all, thinks Paul. His headache has all but gone and he feels surprising peaceful and relaxed, all things considered.

The sun appears from behind the clouds and the bright light forces Paul to reach for his sunglasses, even though it's four o'clock on a December afternoon. The phone rings.

'Hello Paul, old boy. It's me, Jim Parker - I hope you don't mind me calling you on a Friday afternoon, when all good men and true should be enjoying their first snifter.'

Jim Parker. A head-hunter Paul had once known, but never met.

Parker operated entirely by telephone from his home in the country, giving the impression of enormous secrecy, top-level connections and hidden depths of inside knowledge, none of which he ever actually revealed. He reminded Paul of a slightly raffish army officer or gentleman thief - an image drawn from old British films, placing Parker somewhere between Leslie Phillips and Terry Thomas.

I haven't heard from Jim Parker for at least 10 years, thinks Paul, and he was ancient then. He must be in his late-80s by now, at the very least. What a shame that the poor old sod still has to scrape a living like this.

'Great to hear from you, Jim. I'm actually on the road, heading back home. How are you?'

'Still struggling on regardless, old boy,' splutters Parker, his whisky and tobacco encrusted voice barely functioning. 'How wonderful to hear your dulcet tones again, after all these years. How the devil are you?'

'I'm still here at RLA, doing God's work', says Paul. 'I've been here three years now - but it feels like an eternity.'

'Funny you should mention it, old boy', croaks Parker. 'That's just why I'm calling. A truly fascinating job has come across my desk and I immediately thought of you. It's a kind of right-hand man role, reporting directly to someone really rather important. I can't give you a name just now, but let's just say that he's well-known for working in mysterious ways, at a global level. The money won't be an issue and trust me, this is a role that will really give you the chance to spread your wings.'

'That sounds absolutely amazing, Jim. I'd love to talk about it - but now is not really the time. Can I call you back when I get home?'

'Of course you can, old boy. God speed.'

Paul smiles. Despite himself, he is flattered by Parker's call. Right-hand man? Mysterious ways? Spread his wings? He is intrigued. His talent has been recognised. Maybe his star is in the ascendent, at last.

Like the weather, the road conditions have also improved. There are more lanes, less traffic and driving is absolutely effortless. People in other cars are smiling and some wave at Paul. An attractive woman in a Mercedes convertible blows him a kiss. Without thinking, he waves back. She smiles.

The sky is now cloudless and blue, with the sun shining down onto to palm trees and a sparkling blue sea in the distance. It's certainly not Rutland Water, the nearest large expanse of water he can think of - perhaps I took a wrong turn somewhere? It looks more like Southend, but the locals are too attractive and friendly.

The thought soon passes. Wherever he is, it's a lot better than Leeds on a wet, cold Friday. His headache has now completely gone, replaced by a euphoric feeling of well-being and happiness.

The phone rings again. It's Ryder. He engages Paul in some lightweight but surprisingly enjoyable banter, conducted at a relatively low volume. Apparently, Laura has called him and has decided to take a job in Glasgow, starting immediately after the New Year break.

'Or Hogmanay as she would probably call it', he jokes (possibly for the first time ever, thinks Paul).

So that's Laura out of the picture, thank goodness. And there's more good news: Trevor Helliwell has called Ryder to apologise for sitting on the contract, which he has now signed and sent by email.

'He speaks very highly of you, Paul, and wants to talk about some big new projects. I knew I could count on you to build a good relationship with him and as I've always said, you've got a great future with us.'

Ryder has also spoken with Paul's other major client, Sara Williams of the Harwich Group, who he saw at an industry function. Over a drink, Williams had sung Paul's praises and spoken enthusiastically about the future. The Harwich Group is expanding fast, with some new acquisitions in the pipeline, which will require RLA's involvement.

They exchange festive greetings, with Ryder word-perfect on the names of Paul's wife and child.

Maybe Ryder isn't such a bad guy after all, thinks Paul as he rings off. Perhaps I should invite him and his wife round for dinner? Maybe even ask him to be Godfather to Nathan. He imagines the five of them, strolling happily by the seaside, and smiles.

Perhaps a father figure is what he needs. He lost both his own parents years ago and thinks of them now, smiling sadly. If there is some sort of after-life, it would be great to see them again. Paul has always been an atheist, if he ever thought about such things at all, but now he feels a strong conviction that something like that might be possible.

The thought makes him happy. In fact, he can't stop smiling. Life is good. The window is down and a warm breeze is blowing off the ocean. He has no idea where he is or where he's going, but wherever it is, it seems like somewhere he was destined to be, the best of all possible worlds.

He turns the music back up. A road sign, illustrated with a knife and fork motif, tells him that the next exit, St Peter's Gates, is one mile away. 'Good, a service station', thinks Paul. He's bursting for a pee and is feeling a little peckish. His phone beeps and he glances at the message: 'Steak and chips tonight, red wine open, C U later. S xxx.'.

Paul smiles. All his problems have been solved. His assistant is out of the way, never to return. His clients love him. Next year's business is in the bag. He has been headhunted and a fantastic new job as right-hand man to someone mysterious and powerful is as good as his, if he wants it. His wife is cooking his favourite meal tonight.

The sun is shining in a cloudless blue sky as he slows down and takes the exit carefully, singing loudly.

'Highway to Hell' he screams, 'I'm on the highway to hell.'

VI

Quarter-Pounder and Spike are standing on the hard shoulder of the motorway in the darkness, picking gingerly through the wreckage of a smouldering car.

They never made their party. No sooner had they turned onto the A52 than control had sent them back down the M1 to a road traffic incident.

An ambulance is pulling away, as they stand bathed in blue and orange lights from the various emergency and recovery vehicles. A cold wind blows snow across the tyre tracks of the crashed vehicle.

'Poor bastard didn't stand a chance', says Spike, blowing into his hands and stamping his feet.

'Control say that he swerved across two lanes of traffic and ploughed into the back of that lorry at 90 miles an hour. They reckon the silly sod must have fallen asleep at the wheel. Talk about jam sandwich time. A hell of a way to spend Christmas.'

'Rotten taste in music, too', says Quarter-Pounder, holding up a blackened CD case. 'Who listens to AC/DC these days?'

LOOK ME IN THE EYE

I

'I have to confess that, like Winston Churchill, I love pigs. As the great man once said, a cat looks down on a man, a dog looks up to a man, but a pig will look a man in the eye and see his equal.'

James Arnold pauses, chuckling to himself. In his early sixties, he has the look of a man who has been enjoying too much food for rather too long. Someone who, having been poured into his clothes, forgot to say when. His unkempt beard hides a multitude of chins. But this is radio, so there are no limits to his self-confidence.

'I'm here today to tell you that while pigs may well be my equals, I love nothing better than eating them. There is no part of a pig that I do not absolutely relish: from their nose to their tail, from their cheeks to their trotters, and from their succulent offal to their crispy ears. Not to mention more traditional meals like a roasted joint with its crackling and lashings of gravy, a pork chop with apple sauce, or the humble sausage and mash. I'll be back with more after the break.'

'Thank you, James, that was absolutely mouth-watering,' says Sally Owen, the presenter, from her seat on the other side of the desk, almost sounding as though she meant it. 'But now, over to Alexander Gough for the Ten o'clock news here on Radio Anglia. More from James Arnold, our very own food expert, right after the break.'

'It's all going rather well, isn't it,' says Arnold confidentially, shuffling in his seat whilst adjusting his shirt tails, underpants, a layer of stomach and, quite probably, his genitals, all in one practiced manoeuvre.

'Now then, how about a cup of tea, my dear?' he says, turning to the young woman in black jeans, T-Shirt and Doc Marten boots, huddled in the corner of the small studio.

'Err, I don't think we've met,' she manages to stutter, 'I'm Tracey Melrose, BBC trainee and today's producer.'

'Yes, yes,' booms Arnold, looking at her tattoos with obvious distaste. 'Milk and no sugar, please. And some biscuits if you have them.'

Before she can respond, it's time for the programme to resume. Arnold is soon back in his stride. The fat old sod loves pigs almost as much as he loves himself, thinks Tracey.

'The pig is the undoubted king of farm animals and I'll take on any man who disagrees with me. Or woman, of course. I'll take the knee for beef and lamb - their lives matter, as do their glorious and very necessary deaths - but no other meat is anywhere near as versatile as Pork. The skin, the fat, the salt cure - the sheer magnificent *piggyness* of it all.'

He pauses, a dreamy look in his eyes.

'As I said before the news, every part of a pig can be eaten, from tip to toe. All of it. Nothing left but the squeak, as they used to say. The joints and the cuts, of course; pork belly in all its crunchy, fatty glory; and the many products that can be made from cooked and cured pork, like our wonderful local pies and sausages, and the magnificent charcuterie, chorizo, Iberico ham, salami and salchichon that our European friends produce.'

Pausing for effect and, one suspects, to sponge drool from his beard, Arnold rubs his hands enthusiastically and continues.

'Take *andouillettes*, for example.' He rolls the word around his mouth like a fine wine, the better to demonstrate his *savoir faire*. 'A simple peasant food perhaps, but can you possibly think of a better, a more noble, use for pig's tripe?'

Sally has no option but to shake her head and hope that he keeps talking. Noble? She doesn't know exactly what tripe is, let alone what to use it for, but feels instinctively that it is something revolting that she would definitely draw the line at cooking, let alone eating. She and Tracey exchange fake-vomiting faces out of Arnold's sight. Oblivious, he keeps talking, clearly enthused by his subject.

'Tripe is the lining of a pig's stomach, my dear,' he continues. 'I can't recommend it highly enough. Perhaps I'll cook it for you one evening.'

A further exchange of faces take place. It wouldn't much matter what he cooks, think Sally and Tracey as one, the idea of being in such an intimate setting with him was utterly repulsive. Undaunted, Arnold resumes.

'And even if you don't like Pork as the main course, as it were - and I can see from the faces of my colleagues here that they're not too keen on some of my more epicurean suggestions - the fact is that there is no savoury dish that cannot be improved by the addition of a little bit of pig – *un soupcon de cochon*, so to speak. Take lardons, for example, those little cubes of pink beauty that can transform soups, salads, stews, coq au vin, quiches - and the list goes on. If you'd like to know more, may I recommend my rather splendid new book - *James Arnold's Pig Adventures* - available in all good bookstores now.'

'But what about the pigs themselves, James?' asks Sally, 'What do they eat?'

'A very good question, Sally,' patronises Arnold, in his cultivated fruity tones. 'Well, pigs will eat just about anything - and back in the day, that's exactly what they were given. Household scraps, you name it. It's a little more scientific than that these days, of course, and they are given carefully-managed diets to ensure optimum health and happiness. But they are still omnivores, and will eat anything, given the chance - even humans.'

Arnold smiles, savouring the shocked and disgusted faces of his studio audience.

'Don't worry - they don't go hunting us down. But it is well-known that if pigs are hungry enough and there is a dead human body to hand, they will eat it. Quickly, too. Flesh, internal organs, bones - the lot. Everything except teeth. They don't like teeth. Anyway, most pigs are far too well looked after for anything like that to happen - which brings us neatly to next week, does it not Sally?'

'Indeed it does, James. Yes, next week we will be broadcasting live from Eastleigh Farm, Suffolk's largest organic free-range pig farm. James, Tracey and I will be there, wearing our best wellies, talking to owner David Moody, who will be launching a new range of sausages on an unsuspecting world.'

'I'm really looking forward to that. Let's hope he's got plenty of free samples,' adds Arnold, bringing his piece to an end.

'And that concludes my modest bow - nay, genuflection - to the sheer majesty of the pig, the king of farm animals. Versatile, inexpensive - and, in the right hands, absolutely delicious. All that, and I haven't even mentioned the good old bacon sandwich - a pleasure that I hope to enjoy very shortly.'

He laughs uproariously, sits back in his seat and gently breaks wind, politely raising one buttock as he does so. After all, one does have standards.

Sally takes over, relieved to be changing subject. 'Thank you so much, James Arnold. Who would have thought that pigs could be so interesting? And don't forget, James will be back with us next week, checking out David Moody's sausages. We've got traffic news coming up soon here on Radio Anglia, but first, here's an oldie from Blur.'

As Park Life plays, Sally shakes James' hand, managing to head off his attempt at a kiss, and gratefully lets Tracey usher him out of the studio.

'I think the canteen does bacon sandwiches,' she says, 'but I've got to carry on working I'm afraid.'

'Not to worry, my dear. I quite understand.' And with that, off he waddles, sniffing the air hungrily. Over the station speakers, Blur are still playing.

'You should cut down on your pork life mate, get some exercise.'

'At least I've still got my old DJ skills,' thinks Sally, smirking to herself.

II

'He doesn't get any better, I'm afraid,' says Sally. 'Is there no food stuff so foul that he won't absolutely wallow in it? He was really getting off on some of that guts and tripe stuff, I reckon. Personally, I found some of it so repulsive I almost spewed. And I don't turn my nose up at much food these days.'

The morning show finished, Sally and Tracey are having their customary debrief over a cup of coffee. Sally is now classed as a veteran presenter, as she is in her fifties. Having built a career upon flirtatious deference to male colleagues and guests, and the enthusiastic use of double-entendres, she feels more vulnerable than most to the twin forces of ageism and sexism.

Her cause is not helped, she thinks, by the weight she has acquired during her years at Radio Anglia. It shouldn't matter, but when her (female) boss regularly asks about her health, in exaggerated tones of concern, she can see which way the wind is blowing. She re-arranges the voluminous pashmina which is enveloping her entire upper body in a doomed attempt to disguise her bulk and turns to Tracey.

'What did you make of him, Trace? Not ideal for your first week as stand-in producer, I'd have thought.'

'No, not ideal,' says Tracey. 'Particularly as I'm a veggie. And a vegan. So the idea of eating any form of meat - or anything meat-related - is absolutely abhorrent to me, let alone the idea of breeding animals for slaughter. But it's not just that - it's him as well. The way he adjusts his balls and sniffs, snorts and farts all the time. He might as well have rooted and snuffled as well, the pig.'

Tracey sips at her coffee and continues.

'And the way he talks to us - just expecting me to get his coffee, because I'm female, for example. I thought that wasn't even a thing anymore. He's only a paid employee, the same as us, isn't he?'

'I don't think he is actually. He's got some sort of deal where he does it for free, as long as he's allowed to plug his books and so on. Which he does, as you may have noticed.'

'Either way, he's a pig. And I really, really don't like him. People like him need to be taught a lesson.'

'Why not come over to the Dive Bar for a drink at lunchtime and we can talk about it. I'm meeting an old friend, but I've got a feeling you'll get on rather well.'

III

The Dive Bar, Bury St Edmund's only surviving wine bar, is located underneath the mediaeval town hall and accessed by a steep staircase round the side of the building. In the 1980s, it was considered a smart place to be: now, it is older, shabbier and just about hanging on in there, like most of its clientele.

Arnold, who is a regular, is holding court at the bar with a small group of friends. Like him, they are escapees from London, now pursuing an ever-more elusive dream of a more artisan, more independent existence. This means that they usually have a lot to grumble about, which is why they meet here, every Friday lunchtime.

They are discussing David Moody's new low-fat sausage brand, which promises 'All the pig, all the taste, half the calories'. Alan Perry, who used to be a currency dealer in the City and now runs a specialist cheese shop in Market Street called the Grand Fromage, is addressing the others. In his early fifties, he is running to fat, with thinning dark hair slicked back over his large head.

'I've never been too sure about these products that claim to offer all of this, but none of that,' he says, smoothing back his sparse hair with one hand, wine glass in the other. 'They never seem to work for me. I've been trying some of these low alcohol drinks - let's face it, after 25 years in the city, I needed to dry out a bit.'

He takes a large gulp of his wine, looks at the glass ruefully, and continues. 'The trouble is, we don't all want to start drinking glasses of weird alcohol-free concoctions made from rare herbs and exotic fruits by bearded hipsters in Hoxton or yummy mummies with rich hubbies in West London. We just want to drink beer that tastes like beer, but with less alcohol. And the fact is, most of these low alcohol beers taste like piss. I don't suppose Moody's sausages will be much different.'

There were nods all round. Age and experience had taught them to be sceptical about advertising and marketing claims and promises, to the point of extreme cynicism.

Arnold takes over. 'Here's a good one for you. Did I ever tell you about the Churkey?' He looks around with a glint in his eye and carries on before anyone could speak.

'Well, when I was in Fleet Street, many years ago now, I was sent to a lavish product launch at the Cafe Royal. No expense spared.' 'So there we all are, knocking back the free bubbly like there's no tomorrow, when these buglers from the Royal Household Cavalry blast out a fanfare. And into the room, borne aloft on a silver platter, enters this bloody great chicken that has somehow become the size of a monstrous turkey. All the tasty breast meat, none of the bone – you get the idea.'

He pauses for a drink, allowing Tony Watkins, the owner of Café Society, an artisan coffee shop, to interject. Once an accountant, Watkins now counts coffee beans and measures frothy milk in his steamy lair next to the public toilets.

'Anyone for another?' he asks. 'My shout. Denise? Alan? James? OK, I'll get another bottle of the house plonk. Sorry, James, do carry on.'

'Anyway,' continues Arnold, 'once we'd all sat through the presentation and drunk ourselves stupid, we were each given a Churkey to take away. I took mine back home at the weekend and Mother cooked it for Sunday lunch. She wasn't a bad cook, but it tasted absolutely fowl - pardon the pun - and we had to throw it away.'

'Not surprisingly,' concluded Arnold, 'the product never made it into the shops and to this day, ancestors of the Churkey are said to roam East Anglia. Massive bloated birds are sometimes sighted waddling across fields, scaling fences and scaring children.'

'So another 'all of this and none of that' product bites the dust,' says Watkins, laughing politely. 'It's not looking good for Moody, is it?'

'All the taste and half the fat? I like a bit of fat in my sausage personally,' cackles Denise Bloom coarsely, taking a large swill of her wine with practiced ease.

Denise runs an upmarket flower shop in the town called, unsurprisingly, Blooms. No-one is quite sure what she did in London and everyone is too frightened to ask, but she still exudes an air of faded glamour and potential availability that men of a certain age are attracted to.

'But let's not be too quick to condemn,' she adds. 'You never know what the slimy shit might have up his sleeve. And talk of the devil...'

At that moment, David Moody enters the Dive Bar, smiling broadly at the small group of happy drunks waving at him from the bar. Tall, dark and unshaven, he looks what he is - a wealthy man in his late forties, pretending to be a farmer.

'I haven't seen so many happy faces since I fed the pigs this morning. No offence intended, Denise,' he adds, bending to kiss her fragrant upturned cheek. 'And yes please, a glass of what you're all having would be great. It looks like it's done the trick for you lot.'

'We were just talking about your sausages, David. Anything new to report? Have Tesco been on the phone with a big order?'

'No, but I am hoping to hear from a certain celebrity chef who's interested in getting involved. I can't give you a name just yet, I'm afraid. That will help me to emphasise the food quality aspects of the product. The animal welfare and soil association accreditations are already taken care of, I'm glad to say.'

Arnold, leaning at the bar, carefully wipes his beard, which has taken some punishment from the olives he has been eating, and prepares to hold forth.

It's time to take command of the gathering by unleashing a salvo of tried and tested anecdotes from the Arnold archives, loosely tailored to the subject under discussion.

'I've come across a few of those celebrity chefs in my time, let me tell you. I'm not surprised they're keen to get involved – they're all going bust, left, right and centre. Look at that idiot, Jamie Oliver. Gurning away on television while his restaurant empire crashes and burns - and then he has the cheek to blame it all on excessive costs and market conditions. If you ask me, he's just cashed in on his name, taken the money and run. Except it turns out there is no money.' Arnold shakes his head, snorts in disgust and takes a long pull of his wine.

'You've got to feel a bit sorry for the punters lured into these places,' interjects Denise, pushing back her long dark hair. 'After all, he's got a lot going for him, has young Jamie - that cheeky mockney thing, his cooking skills and a real love of food - not a bad combination. I'd certainly be up for it if he had a restaurant here.'

She fields the inevitable sexist 'banter' from her four friends and continues.

'But I'd know it's all bound to end in tears. Jamie won't have been anywhere near the restaurant since the official opening, let alone the kitchen. And even when he was in town, he wasn't there for long – he probably kept the engine of his car running while he was in the restaurant, so he could make a quick getaway. It's just another chain restaurant - but with a brand built around Jamie, who's never there, run by staff who barely know how to eat with a knife and fork. It's doomed from the start. Is it him you're signing-up David, by the way?'

'No, it's not him, thank God,' smiles Moody.

'Is it Gordon Ramsey?' asks Perry. 'I've got to admit, I've got a sneaking admiration for that guy. He might have a face like an elephant's scrotum, but he tells it like it is and really knows his stuff. I mean, picture the scene: he wanders into a restaurant owned and run by a pair of clueless incompetents. Tumbleweed is blowing across the empty tables, the place is covered in cobwebs and they are close to bankruptcy. Enter Gordon, who - despite being the only customer - gets slow service and revolting, badly-cooked food which he spits onto to the floor in disgust.'

Moody picks up the baton. 'And no, it's not Gordon Ramsey, either. But I agree with you – I love that show: you know, the chef and Gordon hate each other on sight and have a shouting match, inevitably involving a lot of bad language. As far as I'm concerned, these lousy places deserve as much profanity, spittle and halitosis as he's prepared to give them.'

'I could do that,' says Arnold, spotting a much-needed career opportunity. 'I could do that show. After all, I've got whatever Gordon's got.'

'Well, you've certainly got the halitosis, darling,' says Denise, to laughter all round, patting Arnold's arm and whispering 'only joking' to pacify him.

'No, I mean it,' says Arnold. 'I may not be a celebrity chef, but I am a reasonably well-known food writer. That's more than that potato-headed arse, Greg Wallace - he was just a vegetable salesman and now he's all over the place, shouting his oikish mouth off about food, cooking and all sorts of things he knows bugger all about.'

Arnold pauses for a refreshing glug of wine, possibly to replenish the vitriol he has used, and continues. 'There's a never-ending procession of those sorts of food programme on television - it's only one step up from restaurant reviews and goodness knows, I've done enough of those. In fact, I've got some funny stories for you on that subject.'

Arnold stops for encouragement and, receiving none, carries on anyway.

'A few of us on the old Evening News in London used to share out the restaurant reviews, under the collective pen name of Colin Cullimore. It meant a free meal every so often and some sport when you came to write the review. We used to compete to see who could slip in the most damning comments - it was all great fun and amazing what you could get away with in those days. I have to admit that it felt good to have so much power over the success of a business, let me tell you. I've heard that a few of them took quite a financial hit as a result. But like you said David, some of these places deserve it.'

And so the afternoon continues, more wine flows, and the conversation meanders pleasantly. Arnold is as happy as it is possible for a man of his age and type to be. He is half-pissed, well on the way to being fully pissed, talking with convivial companions who appear to appreciate his company and opinions, and standing next to an increasingly attractive woman who is leaning against him in what he hopes is a provocative manner.

He was far too pre-occupied to notice Sally and Tracey sitting at a table around the corner of the bar, deep in conversation with a third person.

IV

'So what brings you up to sleepy Suffolk, Melanie?' asks Tracey, swigging from a bottle of Porker's Suffolk Cider. You can't avoid pigs in this town, it seems.

Sally's friend, Melanie Haslam, is a detective with the Metropolitan Police. They'd shared a flat in Battersea back in the 80s when Sally was a young journalist with IPC. Like Arnold, after a few years of unrealised potential in London, Sally had taken the well-trodden path to provincial obscurity.

'I'm actually up here for work' replies Melanie. 'But somehow I've managed to stretch it into a weekend break. And that doesn't happen very often, I can tell you, not with the shift patterns we get at the Met.'

After a discussion about Melanie's accommodation (an Air B&B in a nearby village), her partner (also in the Met) and their plans for the weekend (food, drink and chilling-out seem to be high on the list), Sally asks her about the work that brought her here.

'We had a new lead on a case we closed a few years back' replies Haslam. 'Quite by chance, we found out that someone we've been looking for may have moved to this area, so I'm here to follow it up, shake a few trees and see what falls out.'

'Sounds exciting,' says Tracey. 'Please tell us more - this could be a big story in this part of the world.'

'Unfortunately, it will all have to be off the record for now,' replies Haslam. 'But you'll be the first to know, I promise. There was this woman who nearly beat someone to death and then managed to disappear before we could charge her or take her to court.'

'So there could be a murderer, living right here in Bury St Edmunds,' says Sally, slightly shocked at the idea, despite herself.

'Well, not quite a murderer - although it was close' replies Haslam. 'She used to run a restaurant in Hampstead, which had been open for a year or so and was really starting to take off. Then, it got a particularly cruel and damning review in a newspaper, it all spiralled downhill quite quickly, and eventually the restaurant had to close. She blamed a friend of a friend, who was a journalist, and attacked him with a hammer.'

'Poor woman. I don't blame her. What did the journalist write?'

'Among other things, he described the restaurant as an overpriced tarts boudoir serving lacklustre food with no flavour. And that was just the start - he said that the waitress was clueless, overweight and rude. It was the owner's night off, but she assured us that the lady in question was a librarian and beyond reproach.'

'That wasn't very nice. It sounds like he deserved a bit of a thumping,' says Sally.

'The trouble is the guy she attacked couldn't possibly have written the piece. Not only was he on holiday at the time, but he didn't even work for the Evening News, the paper that printed the review. By the time he'd regained consciousness - he was in a coma for two weeks - and we'd found out what had happened, she'd closed the restaurant and vanished without trace. Until now.'

'So why's she here, Mel? And how did you find her?'

'We've learned a bit about her since the attack - she's called Diana Burgess, she had blonde hair cut into a bob, and she had bipolar disorder. Now, you can change your name, your job, your hairstyle and your hair colour, but you will still be mentally ill - and we discovered that the psychiatrist that used to treat her in London has moved to a clinic up here. So that's my first port of call tomorrow.'

'We need to find her,' continues Haslam. 'She's a dangerous woman - the journalist she attacked was an innocent man and will never fully recover. I dread to think what she might do to someone who's actually guilty.'

V

It's the morning of the sausage launch. Arnold surveys the audience, standing before him in the muddy and odiferous yard of Eastleigh Farm holding glasses of champagne. God, he loves an audience - and this one seems to like him, too. Ah well, time to draw this to a close.

'And in conclusion, I'd like to commend David Moody's unique and laudable dedication to rearing the finest organic free-range pigs in the East of England - from rare and endangered breeds, at that. It's this dedication that provides the soundest possible base for the wonderful new product we are here today to celebrate. Once upon a time, sausages were a guilty pleasure for some of we more health-conscious consumers.'

He pats his bulging waistcoated stomach proudly and carries on.

'But now, thanks to the dedication of one man and his team of pork experts, even the most extreme dieter can enjoy a sausage whenever it takes his or her fancy. All this from a man who, until a few years ago, was running a successful technology company. Ladies and Gentlemen, I give you Moody's Low Fat Organic Sausages. All the pig, all the taste, half the fat.'

His speech concluded, Arnold waves his champagne glass in the air before tipping the contents down his throat. The audience applaud politely and drain their glasses, which are inexpertly topped-up by a team of young girls from the local college, wearing short black skirts, tight white blouses and badly-applied make-up.

David Moody runs onto the makeshift stage - an old trailer - and takes over at the microphone. 'Thank you so much, everyone - and thank you for stepping in at the last minute, James. We are fortunate indeed to have someone of your calibre here today.'

Arnold bows his head in acknowledgement and simulates modesty. He is keen to convey that a man of his status would only do this sort of thing as a massive favour to an old friend and not because some third-rate chef had dropped out that same morning. He would be interviewing Moody for his radio programme, of course, but that would imply that he was an impartial professional, not a paid-for stooge.

Sally and Tracey, both wearing Radio Anglia fleeces and armed with a microphone and digital recorder respectively, are working the crowd, looking for someone interesting to interview. Melanie Haslam is with them, all business in a black trouser suit, also looking for a person of interest. Arnold weaves into view, still glowing from his moment of fame.

'I hope you ladies managed to record my little speech,' he asks, as one of the young waitresses refills his glass until it overflows. 'Thank you, my dear,' he leers, examining her carefully from top to toe.

Why not pin a rosette on her while you're at it, thinks Tracey, as she responds to his rather unnecessary question. What else did he think they were doing?

'Yes James, we've got your speech, loud and clear. And a few photos for the website as well. By the way, have you met Sally's friend, Melanie Haslam? She's here looking for an escaped lunatic.'

'Not exactly a lunatic,' says Haslam, shaking Arnold's paw-like hand. 'We can't use that sort of language these days. I think the correct term is mentally-challenged potential crime victim.'

'Victim?' exclaims Sally. 'She nearly killed an innocent man.'

'But she was also a victim. Whoever wrote that restaurant review will be charged with committing a hate crime and could end up getting a longer sentence than she does.'

Sally raises her eyes skywards and asks, 'By the way, Mel, did you find that psychiatrist?'

'Yes, but sadly he hasn't seen Diane Burgess since before the attack. He did tell me something interesting though. He was responsible for signing-off her medication until he moved here. It was pretty powerful stuff, apparently - and unless she has found another psychiatrist, she will have run out by now. And that means that she should, by law, be sectioned until she is under the grip of new medication.'

'According to the psychiatrist,' Haslam continues, 'once she stops taking the meds, she could be tipped over the edge into a murderous frenzy at any time. She was bad enough when she was taking them, but now - she's a walking timebomb.'

'A five-star fruitcake, you mean,' adds Arnold, walking away in search of another drink.

VI

A few hours later and the product launch has become a smaller, more friendly, and definitely more drunken, gathering. The Dive Bar crowd are all present and correct, David Moody's free drinks continue to flow, and the waitresses have been sent home for their own safety.

Like everyone else, Denise is more than a little tipsy.

'Pigs are so sweet, aren't they? They're absolutely adorable. I hate the idea of eating them, it's so barbaric.'

'It is indeed barbaric,' says Arnold. 'But so are many other things - and they're all quite delicious too. David's pigs are well cared for and have a good life right up until the very last moment. They never know what's hit them - and that's more than most of us will be able to say. When my times comes, I'm not buggering off to Switzerland - I'm coming here.'

'Do you think he'd let me see them?' asks Denise.

'I'm sure he would – David's got nothing to hide. I'd be happy to escort you, if you like. Most of them are out in the fields, but there are some over there, in that building behind the offices.'

Denise takes his arm - mainly because she can barely stand - and they totter off towards the isolation building behind the farm offices. Arnold opens the door and stands back to allow her to enter. She is greeted by a blast of warmth, a heady aroma, and a lot of excited grunting and squealing. It reminds her of a nightclub she used to go to in her teens. About a dozen extremely large pigs are standing in an iron-fenced straw-festooned enclosure.

'Not exactly Pinky and Perky, I'm afraid, but *voila* - pigs,' says Arnold expansively.

'But if these pigs are indoors, in a pig pen, how can they be described as free range?' asks Denise, her head clearing for a minute.

'These are David's stormtroopers' explains Arnold. 'An elite regiment. These are the boars - the male pigs - selected for his breeding programme. They've all been on a special high-protein diet and now they're on a 24-hour fast until tomorrow, to optimise sperm quality and to stop them getting lazy. They'll spend the night here and then, in the morning, they'll be released into the fields to service as many sows as they can manage, before coming back here for a slap-up feed and a good kip. I must admit, it all sounds rather good to me.'

'And to me,' purrs Denise, leaning against Arnold.

'Please be careful, my dear. They can get a bit aggressive because they're hungry, so don't go too near. And they're a little frustrated, because they're all geared up for their important work tomorrow. They're fully locked and loaded, you might say - just look at the size of their, uhm, round Gentleman's parts.'

'Their balls, you mean,' says Denise. 'And don't worry darling, I like a man with a bit of aggression. It brings out the beast in me. And I share their frustration. How about you?'

She is now wrapped around Arnold, too tightly for him to ignore, her intentions increasingly clear. He is unable to do more than grunt in reply.

'I say darling,' says Denise. 'I've got an idea.'

She leads Arnold into a covered area next to the pens, a holding bay for the pigs as they come and go. She starts kissing his face and pushes him hard against the railing. He smells her perfume, feels her large breasts against his even larger stomach and starts to rise to the occasion.

'I enjoyed your radio programme last week, darling,' she whispers, breathing into his ear. 'Are pigs really omnivores?'

'Absolutely. Especially when they're hungry. Everything but the teeth,' he mumbles, his hands working overtime.

Arnold is trembling like a teenage boy now, loosening her clothing and reaching eagerly for her breasts. The truth is that no woman has been this keen on him for as long as he can remember.

She is still pushing herself against him, forcing him to lean backwards, right over the railing.

'Oh yes, I really loved your last programme, James. In fact, I love all your stories. Especially that one you told us all in the wine bar the other day, about the restaurant reviews you used to write. You know, the ones where you all competed to write the most damning and hurtful reviews. That really turned me on.'

She gives him one final push. He overbalances and falls backwards into the pen, landing on his back and hitting his head hard on the concrete floor.

Denise looks down at him. Lust has been replaced by hatred. Her face now ugly and contorted with rage, she is shouting angrily. 'That was MY restaurant, you bastard. I lost everything. Now we're even.'

James Arnold is lying in a pool of his own blood, losing consciousness.

The last thing he sees before blacking out is the face of a pig, looking him in the eye.

VII

'This is Radio Anglia News. Good morning, I'm Alexander Gough.'

'A set of human teeth found in a pig enclosure at Eastleigh Farm, Benlake, have been identified as belonging to James Arnold, 61, a local food writer and radio presenter. He had been at the farm for a promotional event and was reported missing the following day.'

MAN WALKS INTO PUB

I

As soon as I saw the sign above the door, I knew that I had no choice but to walk in.

I'm not much of a pub man. My Dad and brother were active participants in pub culture, with a detailed understanding of the rules and rituals involved. Who to talk to, who to acknowledge, who to ignore. When to buy a round, when to keep your hand in your pocket. I'm more of an observer: it goes with my analytical nature.

I don't drink much these days and when I do, it's more likely to be wine than beer. I'm not very social, either - I'm happy at home with the wife and a good book or something on the telly. If we do go out, it's for a meal in a restaurant. So normally, I wouldn't walk into any pub, let alone one I hadn't been to before. But for some reason, this evening was different.

It had been a long day. After work, I'd caught the train up to Birmingham from London, arriving at New Street around 7.30. I had an important meeting early the next morning and my plan was to be there, on time and on form. I checked in to my hotel - the Premier Inn in the city centre - and decided to go for a stroll.

It was a warm summer evening and downtown Birmingham seemed a little European, with people strolling about Centenary Square, groups drinking outside bars and the trams clicking and squealing in the background.

Birmingham was busily re-inventing itself, which is why I was there. I work for Ellett & Watkins, a large firm of surveyors based in North London. I've been there for twenty years now, since I left University - they're a decent firm and I'm told that I am well on my way to becoming a partner. We were tendering for a large city centre redevelopment project and my meeting was with the developers, for an initial site visit.

So far, I was excited. Despite my usual cynicism, this city really was going places, certainly compared with what it used to be like.

It would be great for me - personally and professionally - to be involved in a project of this size and importance. If massive new shopping centres and office buildings are your idea of progress, that is.

My walk took me to an older part of the city centre, where the Victorian red and brown brick buildings that had once housed workshops and tradespeople were cut through with narrow streets of terraced houses. I turned a corner, past a large Church, and that's where I saw it. A typical corner pub, with one side on the main road, the other on the side street, and a sign above the door: The Royal Oak.

II

As I said, I felt compelled to go in. I'm not sure why: it's not as though the Royal Oak looked particularly welcoming. It clearly hadn't been decorated for some years, the windows were dirty and the door was badly in need of a coat of paint. Until I saw someone walk in, I thought it was closed.

The inside of the pub wasn't much better. There was a lot of brown wood, most of it covered in worn varnish - in fact, the floor was down to bare splintered wood. Despite this, the pub was surprisingly busy. Groups of people, mainly men, were standing around talking and holding pints, and I weaved my way through them to the bar.

I squeezed between two men sitting at the bar and located a bank note in my wallet - this didn't seem like the sort of place where plastic would be welcomed. The middle-aged man in a yellow cardigan behind the bar greeted me cordially enough and I ordered a pint of best bitter, because that's what my Father and brother would have done. But then, it didn't seem like the sort of place that would have a wine list, either.

Rather gingerly, I took a sip of my pint. It was surprisingly good - orangey in colour, with a slightly frothy head and a nice hoppy tang. I could get a taste for this after all, I thought. I may even have smacked my lips, something I had always thought people only did in ads.

'Not bad, eh?' said the man sitting at the bar, looking up from his newspaper, which was folded to reveal the crossword. He was a few years older than me, quite smartly dressed, with a strong local accent. I won't attempt to replicate that accent here, as it would make fun of people and a city that I very much like.

'No, not bad at all', I said, reading the pump. 'Collymore's Best Bitter. It's new to me, I must admit.'

'Collymore's own the pub', he replied. 'They brew good beer that family. They set up the brewery in the 1850s and were living like aristocrats by the turn of the century, with a chain of pubs right across the city. Great businessmen, but a bunch of greedy bastards, basically.'

'If they're that wealthy, you'd think they could afford to smarten the place up a bit. It's all shabby and no chic, if you know what I mean.' As soon as I opened my mouth, I knew I had put my foot in it.

'Well, it's my local. Seems alright to me,' he said, finishing his cigarette in that way that working men do - holding it between thumb and forefinger and taking a huge final drag, before stubbing it out in the ash tray dismissively. Everyone in the pub was smoking and a cloud of blue-grey smoke hung over the room. After my gaff about the décor, I decided not to comment on this but to make amends instead.

'It seems like a great pub, mind you - a fantastic atmosphere and it's obviously very popular.'

'Oh yes, it's the heart of the community, this pub,' he replied, picking up on my clumsy conversational ploy. 'There's always something going on - we have a great pub quiz, a meat raffle, fancy dress evenings, you name it. And there's a great bunch of blokes come in, we have some good nights here. The trouble is, remember those greedy bastards I mentioned - the Collymore family - there's a rumour that they're going to close the pub and sell it to property developers. Some sort of shopping centre development. We locals are all dead against it, of course, but what we can do? The landowners will always defeat the working man.'

For a moment, I was worried. Was this something to do with me? But I'd read all the documents carefully - we would be working on derelict land, the site of buildings that had all been demolished years ago.

By now, it was time for a second pint and this time I bought my new friend one. I never check my change, but as I put it back into my pocket, it seemed a decent amount. I remember thinking that the prices seemed very reasonable here.

He raised his pint glass and looked up at me from his stool, a slight smile on his stubbly face and his dark eyes creasing.

'Cheers. I'm Jim Rigg, by the way. I've got a place over the road - tools, hardware, that sort of thing. It's a family business, we've been here since the 1860s. I'm hoping my son will take it over from me, but he doesn't seem that interested. A lot of the people here are like that - family businesses, fathers and sons, going back generations. This pub is even older, I believe – all the way back to when this area was in the country. It was just a small village then.'

'If it's that old, there must be a few ghosts around,' I joked, trying to change the subject from a boring local history lecture. 'I'm Jon, by the way. Jon Proctor.'

'Well Jon, I have heard a few stories, as it happens' replied Rigg. 'The landlord once told me that it's written into his lease with the brewers that the window at the top of the stairs must always be kept open, no matter what. Strange things happen otherwise, apparently. The story is that some children were killed in a fire before the war - they couldn't get out of the building because all the doors and windows were locked.'

'What sort of strange things, exactly?' I asked.

'They say you can hear footsteps, scratching on the doors, children crying. Things moving about, that sort of thing. Some people feel a hand on their shoulder, but when they turn around there's no one there. Of course, I don't believe in that sort of thing myself.'

At that precise moment, I felt a hand on my shoulder and flinched. I turned around, but no-one was there. Rigg sat there laughing at my obvious surprise, having put his arm right round my back to tap me on my further shoulder. An old schoolboy trick, but it worked. His laugh turned into a serious smokers cough and as he coughed, I got a whiff of his breath, tainted by the distinctive aroma of Cheese & Onion Crisps, the Smith's packet with its little blue bag sitting on the bar in front of him.

'Got you there, Jon' he said, still laughing. 'Just off to the Gents.'

While he was gone, I checked my phone. There was no signal, despite our location close to the centre of Birmingham. I drank more of my beer and looked around. Like Jim had said, they seemed a decent bunch of blokes: older men still here after work, late for their tea, some playing darts; younger men having a few drinks before going out for the evening. Everyone seemed to know each other and there was a lot of laughter. A real working man's pub.

I felt at home here: there aren't any pubs like this where I live, not anymore. There aren't many working men either, come to think if it. And it reminded me of my Dad's local, back in the day. I didn't go there much, but it's where he was if we needed him and it's where he was at his happiest.

We even scattered his ashes in the pub garden, near the outside lavs, giving him the respect he deserved and the chance to see his old friends, often several times a night.

III

The evening passed quickly. By now, we were on our fourth pint and had been joined by a group of Jim's friends. I can remember them all, even now: Bob, Henry, Ken, Mick, Rob, Roger, Ted. They were a friendly lot and I felt like I'd known them all for years. Jim was in full flow by now, his tongue loosened by the ale.

'We've had some good times in here, Jon. See that old piano over there?'

Jim pointed towards the back of the pub, where a battered piano stood next to the Ladies. 'Well, there used to be this old boy who came in here and played it now and again. Stan, I think he was called. Hey Bob - that old boy who used to play piano. Was it Stan? Anyway, usually he just tinkled away to himself in the corner and no one paid him any attention. He wasn't even that good, to be honest.'

Rigg paused for a drag on his cigarette, making sure I was paying attention. He knew how to tell a story and had mastered the art of holding an audience's attention.

'One night, a group of us were having a bit of a session and started joining in with him. Singing all the old songs we were - Knees up Mother Brown, you name it. None of us knew the words, but we did our best. Obviously, we kept the old boy supplied with beer - he just couldn't keep up, could he Mick. There were pints lined up right along the top of the piano, he'd never had it so good. Anyway, come closing time, he'd drunk so much he couldn't walk, he just kept falling off the piano stool. Like a jellyfish he was.'

He paused again, taking a pull of his beer and laughing at his own story.

'So two of the boys helped him home – one on either side, his arms round their shoulders. He only lived round the corner, so they sort of dragged him there, left him propped up against the front door, and rang the bell. As they walked away, his wife came out of the house and shouted after them, 'Oi, you lot. Where's his bloody wheelchair?'

Rigg and his mates laughed loudly, as did I. We all drank more beer, while he finished his story.

'Legless, he was. Get it? Of course, we found the wheelchair and took it back, but we never saw him in here again.'

Rigg caught sight of another man, on his way to the Gents, and shouted across to him.

'Oi, Ted. You going to the Villa tomorrow? It's those bloody bluenoses. League match. That's Birmingham City to you, Jon,' he said, turning back to me. 'They're overdue for a good thrashing, that lot. This is a Villa pub, so we'll all be meeting up here for a few pints before the match, if you fancy it.'

I'm not really a football fan. I follow Arsenal, but that's not the same thing at all. I go to matches with the firm when someone drops out at the last minute, and sit in an executive box and drink wine with clients who, like me, don't know any of the players names. The prawn sandwich brigade, to quote Roy Keane. This was different, this was real: it mattered to these men. And now, it mattered to me, as did they, their lives and their pub.

Feeling slightly emotional after a lot more beer than I am used to, I said goodnight, making rash promises about seeing them soon, maybe the football tomorrow, who knows.

Jim shook my hand as I left, looking into my eyes and quietly saying, 'You won't forget us, will you Jon.'

IV

I arrived for my meeting at the Developer's offices early, although a little less bright-eyed than planned. Beer does that, it seems. Luckily, coffee was available in reception and I was in reasonable shape by the time I met Martin and Bob, from the developers, and Janet Hargreaves from the City Council planning department.

They talked me through their plans, explaining how it all fitted into the bigger picture of a more modern, more vibrant Birmingham. I asked some intelligent questions and managed to convey both enthusiasm and competence. And I was genuinely enthusiastic - the more I heard, the more I wanted to be involved with this project. They seemed to have covered all the bases: affordable housing, cycle ways, an extension of the tram network, pedestrianisation and better use of the canals that criss-cross the city. Birmingham has more canals than Venice, as I have been told any number of times.

It was a beautiful morning, so we decided to walk into the city centre, to inspect the site. The sun was shining, reflecting off the windows of the modern office buildings around us. As we walked, the surrounding buildings changed abruptly from tall glass structures to smaller redbrick Victorian shops, houses and warehouses, as we moved into an older part of the city.

'I went to a fantastic pub somewhere round here last night,' I said, seeking to reinforce my credentials with the rather laddish developers. 'Perhaps we could have lunch there later? It's a real old-fashioned local – spit, sawdust, the lot. Great beer too - Collymore's. They were all fanatical Villa fans – told me about the derby match in the league tonight. I might stay an extra night and go along.'

If that didn't endear me to them, then nothing will, I thought. Local knowledge, beer, football. I'm practically a Brummie.

'The pub sounds great, Jon. But I didn't know they still made Collymore's,' said Martin, one of the developers. 'Didn't they sell out to Allied Breweries years ago? Collymore's was my Dad's favourite, back in the day.'

'And I hate to break it to you - but there's no league derby tonight,' added Janet. 'Villa and City haven't been in the same division for years. My partner and I have got season tickets, so I'd know if there was a game.'

'So much for my local knowledge,' I joked. 'I obviously misheard. Beer, football - you'll be telling me I'm wrong about the pub next. See that church spire around the corner, it should be next to that.'

We rounded the corner and saw the church. It was still standing, but was surrounded by waste land, flattened rubble and the foundations of demolished buildings.

'No pub here, sorry mate.' said Martin. 'This is all part of the redevelopment site. The shopping centre will be right over there, the other side of that road - this area here is for the new approach road and service area.'

'This land was bought years ago, some of it speculatively before planning permission had been granted. A lot of it was owned by Collymore's, the brewing family. They didn't want to sell at first, but in the end civic pride got to them.' added Janet.

'Yes, that and the money,' adds Bob. 'Not to mention that old man Collymore was appointed Lord Mayor the following year.'

'Quite a few compulsory purchases were needed,' continued Janet. 'There was a lot of fuss at the time, as it was one of the city's oldest communities. They went down fighting, I have to say. It shouldn't have taken us as long as it did, but you know how it is. Anyway, as you can see, there hasn't been a pub round here for more than 10 years.'

I shrugged my shoulders and held out my hands, in a gesture of apology. 'Sorry, guys. I must have had too many beers last night. The pub is obviously somewhere else altogether. I'm a stranger round here, remember.'

A hand tapped my shoulder. I smelt the familiar aroma of cheese and onion crisps as I swivelled round. No-one was there.

On the corner opposite, I saw a parked bulldozer and a heap of rubbish - they had obviously been clearing and levelling the site. The usual suspects were strewn haphazardly in one corner: a stained mattress, car tyres, broken bottles and some bricks.

And to one side, the remains of an old upright piano and a battered pub sign: The Royal Oak.

PALE MONARCH

I

I'm lying on my back, drifting in and out of consciousness, looking up at a blur of worried faces. I feel strangely at peace. If this is the end, so be it - it's been a blast.

They say that in your final minutes your entire life flashes before you, like a movie. So Max Diesel, one-time rock star - this is your life. Or should I say, was.

II

My mind is not what it once was. Years of abuse can do that. But although I am lying here in a somewhat confused state, some of my early memories are as vivid as a film, even though they're more than 50 years old. Time to get back to where I once belonged.

At an early age, I learned three important things. Being the centre of attention is good and getting paid for it is better. But at the heart of it all, you need God-given talent.

God issued me with my talent at Sunday school, when I was 8 years old. Sunday School took place in the same Church Hall as Wolf Cubs, which I preferred. Every Tuesday evening, we put on our green shirts, scarves and woggles, played games, won badges and sometimes sizzled sausages.

At Sunday School, where I went with my sister, we just said prayers and sang hymns. Then one Sunday, while we were all singing, I was tapped on the shoulder and told to stand at the front.

From now on, I was to be a member of the Church Choir, over the road at the Parish Church. This introduced me to a new world of cassocks, surplices and ruffs, sheet music, harmonies and a small group of strange men with bad breath known as the Tenors and Basses. And best of all, you got paid, in a little brown envelope, with an extra half a crown for weddings. No sausages though.

It's the following year. The church is dark, lit only by the candle I am holding. I had again been singled out, this time to sing at the Christmas Carol service at the Cathedral Church of the Holy Trinity, at the top of the High Street. It is traditional for the first verse of Once in Royal David's City to be sung - solo and unaccompanied - by a boy soprano (in this case, me). I failed to tell my parents about this moment of fame, which I regret to this day.

Fast forward six months. I'm nine years old, sitting in the hallway of a large Victorian house after school. It is silent apart from the loud ticking of the grandfather clock. Dust is visible in the sun streaming through the coloured glass of the windows. The smell is of furniture polish and boiled cabbage. I will spend the next hour singing scales, arpeggios, selecting the middle notes of chords, and avoiding the tobacco-flecked spittle of Mr Barker, my teacher.

The school and my parents had hatched a plan to move me into the big time, by joining the choir of either St Paul's Cathedral or Westminster Abbey. To pass the entrance tests, my parents had paid for me to have singing lessons from Mr Lionel Barker, a retired music teacher. I failed both tests but was offered a place at a 'lesser' cathedral. I don't go, as it also means going away to boarding school, which my Mother didn't want. I was precious.

But for now, this experience gives me all I need - the confidence that I can sing.

III

It's easy to forget just how grey and grim the early seventies were. The swinging sixties had yet to be invented, even though they were in the past. In fact, they probably never happened at all, except for a small group of people in select parts of London. For the rest of us, any 'cultural change' took place very slowly over the course of the next decade.

Before leaving to go full-time with the band, I was at a poly in London for a year, studying social science. Not that I studied much.

The main Poly building was cold, echoing and smelt of wet raincoats and disinfectant. Not that I was there much, preferring to spend most of my time in the student union bar, which was housed in a series of damp railway arches near the Elephant and Castle, like a wartime shelter. Beer was cheap, as were chips, and there was a jukebox, with Quo and the Stones on constant rotation. This was about as good as it got in those days.

Like just about every other male student my age, I had long, greasy hair and wore an old army greatcoat. When I wasn't in the student union, I loped aimlessly around a London that, like my coat, had hardly changed since the end of the war.

There were bombsites for car parks - piles of smashed concrete and old bricks, presided over by limping war veterans. The pavements were broken, so that when you trod on loose paving slabs, water shot up the back of your legs - it had always just rained or was about to.

South of the river, which was where I was based, the entire river frontage was a shabby memorial to the past - the old warehouses and docks in the east, the OXO building, the Nine Elms cold store in Vauxhall and Battersea Power Station. Even the brutal 1950s concrete of the South Bank complex failed to lift the mood, hardly surprisingly.

I know I sound like your Dad - and the way things were back then, it's quite possible that I am - but things were very different then. Three things in particular stick in my mind.

First, how on earth did anything ever happen? Communication was poor: no mobiles or personal computers, just phone boxes with their A and B buttons, and shared phones in the hallways of the large Victorian flat conversions that most people my age seemed to live in.

If you phoned a girl still living at home, you probably had to speak to her parents first - a daunting prospect which must have stopped many a promising romance in its tracks. It all made life – let alone running a band - very difficult.

Second, we were all so unhealthy. Pale, shabby and ungroomed, we all smoked and gave no thought to our diet. I lived on chips, when I remembered to eat at all, and can't remember ever drinking water. We were all as thin as rakes. It's no real surprise that so many of my music industry contemporaries have fallen by the wayside. Not to mention the 'lifestyle issues' so many of us were to face: drink and drugs, of course, as well as venereal diseases (as they were then known).

And finally, we didn't have much in the way of money, clothes or possessions. What little money I had, I hoarded and used for buying records and going to gigs. We could barely afford drink, let alone drugs. We didn't use restaurants. We walked everywhere.

The great thing was music. Life may have been a little miserable, or so it seems now, but the music was great. And our sort of music was everywhere: ballrooms, church halls, dance halls, night clubs, pubs, social clubs, student unions, village halls and youth clubs. To name but a few.

This required a support system of bands, roaming the country in badly-maintained old vans, driving hundreds of miles on a road system that had few motorways, and eating horrible food in cafes and Wimpey bars. I had heard that a good band might get paid £30 for a gig, maybe more. This was exactly the sort of glamorous lifestyle that I was looking for.

Going to a gig was one of the highlights of our lives, but it was rarely easy or comfortable. Often, there wouldn't be a bar in the same room as the band. Listening to the band involved standing or sitting on a dusty wood parquet floor, in a cold room that would smell strongly of cigarette smoke and sweat as it warmed up. Before the band you had come to see, there would be a support band, often inaudible or badly mixed.

When the main band finally appeared, they would be staggeringly loud, often accompanied by the howling and screeching of feedback. After the gig, the pubs would be closed and last buses and trains were few and far between. A long walk home, often in the rain, was involved. And that was a good night out.

IV

It had all started a few years before, at school - a small town grammar school 50 miles outside London. The four us weren't friends, but we came together through a shared interest in music and decided to form a band. How hard could it be?

Chords learned from Bert Weedon's legendary Play in a Day instruction book were painstakingly rehearsed. They say that a whole generation of guitarists learned from that book - Clapton, McCartney, Hank Marvin, Brian May, Pete Townshend and many more. There was no other way to learn, other than from your mates, who weren't much better than you.

Records were listened to, over and over, to work out riffs and chord sequences. Equipment was begged, borrowed, stolen and shared. At our first rehearsal, held in a hut in the grounds of the local mental hospital (as it was then known), my prized Selmer Zodiac 30 watt combo amplifier was somehow used for guitar, bass and vocals.

For our first gig, we hired the back room of a local pub - a low, small room that was nevertheless a regular venue for rock and jazz bands on the outer fringes of the London circuit. The fact that we were all under-age - band and audience - did not seem to matter.

We needed a PA system of some sort for our singer. My girlfriend AT the time persuaded the guy who rented the flat above her parents garage to lend us his amp for the gig. He turned out to be Roy Lynes, the keyboard player for Status Quo, who made us promise not to use it at more than half-volume. He even delivered and collected the amp himself, only for us to turn it up to maximum as soon as he left.

Roy was a lovely man and I got to know him well many years later, when we were touring Australia, where he lived and was playing for fun with a local Quo tribute band.

We decided to look for more bookings. To do this, we needed a name and an image. This was difficult, as we were just four grammar-school boys from nice homes playing any sort of music we could manage.

Eventually, we agreed on the name Pale Monarch. We joked that it had a certain lèse-majesté, a term we had learned in A level history, and commissioned Nigel Bernard, who was good at art, to design a logo. We have used his work - which involved a white skull with red eyes, a crown and gothic script - ever since. And never paid him a bean, I'm ashamed to say.

People often used to ask about our name. We chose it because it was what my Father called me. Whenever I entered a room, he would declaim the words 'Pale Monarch' in stentorian tones of mock importance, and this had made a strong impression on the others in the band.

It was a few years later that I discovered the meaning of the term from my brother. Our Father was a crossword puzzle enthusiast and 'Pale Monarch', it turns out, was a clue for 'Wan King' (or maybe it was the other way round). Either way, it was a subtle, and to him amusing, way of calling his younger son a wanker, which I've had to live with ever since.

The four of us in the band were now a team - all for one, and so on. Jon Thud on drums, Gary Grunter on bass, Mickey Riff on lead guitar. And me, Max Diesel, on lead vocals and rhythm guitar, the frontman and undisputed leader.

These were our stage names, obviously, and so much better than our real names - Jonathan Thomson, Gareth Smith, Michael Richardson and me, Martin Beasant. Names that are redolent of sensible pullovers, the sixth-form chess club and horn-rimmed spectacles.

Pale Monarch were ready to rock. But first, we had to take our A levels.

V

It all got quite serious, very quickly. It was the summer after our A levels. We had established a routine of rehearsals at the mental hospital during the week and a couple of gigs at the weekend - the basement of a local hotel, the back rooms of pubs, tennis clubs, sports and social clubs and birthday parties in village halls.

In a short space of time, we acquired equipment, original material and a manager. All of them a little dodgy, to be honest.

We all had holiday jobs. Gary and I worked at a local lawn mower factory, Jon at his Dad's toy and model shop and Mickey at a warehouse. With the money we were earning - a small fortune, by our standards - we were able to buy more and bigger equipment. Two of the band built enormous PA cabinets from chipboard, which were painted black. The bass player added a massive 'bass bouncer' to his armoury. Suddenly, we were very loud indeed.

We started writing our own songs. It was mainly me, but the others chipped in. The inspiration came from songs we liked which somehow, after a fair amount of incompetent transcription, simplification and new lyrics, became something slightly different.

By the time we'd applied our trademark blend of leaden instrumentation and bellowing vocals, they had become our own songs. Such favourites as Back of the Car Blues, Dirty Woman and Take it From Behind were written during this period. I have always prided myself on my lyrics and had planned to publish them as a book of poetry.

Most importantly, we acquired a Manager. Richard Charles (or Chuck Richards, as he now styled himself) was not an experienced rock group manager, or an experienced anything, but he was very enthusiastic and prepared to work for free. He was part of the little set that had built up around the band, hanging out at rehearsals and supporting us at gigs.

And amazingly, through sheer persistence, he got results: within a few weeks, we were booked up into the following year. More money, better gigs, even a support slot at the local college to a 'name' band - the Chapman Whitney Streetwalkers. This was not one of our better gigs. In fact, it was a disaster. As was the unwritten rule for support bands, we were given no opportunity to sound-check, little time to set-up and a tiny amount of space at the front of the stage, guaranteeing that we played badly and sounded even worse. We learned from this: make sure we're the main act.

To achieve this, we worked our socks off until, by the end of the next year, we were the main act - as long as we played at small venues, anyway. By now, I had given up my Poly course and was in the band full-time. The others did the same, one by one. Our parents were not happy, as you can probably imagine.

You know the rest. We got a record contract with a minor record label. They gave us an advance against royalties, which we promptly spent. After a small amount of success, we were signed by a major label. We now had a routine - make an album, do a tour, make another album, repeat. A single from our first album scraped into the Top Forty for a week and we mimed to it, badly, on a few off-peak regional TV programmes.

It was hard work. A lot of equipment to be loaded in and loaded out, a lot of driving and a constant lack of sleep. Everything to do with the band was disorganised and a little grubby, including the flat we shared, the four of us, the girls we slept with and their underwear. By now, we were all drinking heavily and discovering drugs, interests that the promoters were happy to indulge.

We took full advantage of their generosity, which ensured that we never went on stage sober. Gary tells the story of his visit to a Doctor for a check-up. When asked how much he drank, Gary thought he'd better tone it down a little, as you do, and said: 'oh, not much really - about six pints of beer, a bottle of wine or two, and half a bottle of scotch'. To which the Doctor replied, 'And is that every week?' Leaving Gary with an open goal, 'No, every day'.

Pale Monarch were now quite big. An established third division name, like Howl Howl Howl, West of Suez or Bad Work. Not yet a second division name like Barclay James Harvest, Camel, Caravan or Gentle Giant. But we were well on the way.

Then we went to America.

V1

Our record label believed that we had what it took to succeed in the States, so an American tour was hastily planned. Everything is bigger there, so it was thought at the time, and that certainly applied to our appetite for drink and drugs. To use Nick Lowe's words, every night we would 'ski down mountains of cocaine into lakes of vodka'- or whatever downmarket equivalent was available, in our case. And it was always available.

Girls were also plentiful and not difficult to pick up. In fact, they did all the work. 'I want to take you back to my place and f*ck your brains out' was a typical chat-up line. Even at an industry drinks reception, the wife of one of the record company execs leaned into me and said, 'Just to let you know that every woman in this room wants to f*ck you.' I apologise for the language, but it was them that used it, not me.

Obviously, we hated to disappoint all these lovely ladies and were soon riddled with STDs, lice and cold sores. On top of this, we all had permanent hangovers and were always exhausted because of the amount of travelling and lack of sleep. Inevitably, the band suffered. If all four of us made it on stage at the same time, able to perform at our best, it was a miracle. We played as a three-piece more than once. On one occasion, I was forced to move from frontman to drummer/vocalist, Jon Thud being otherwise disposed, unconscious on the toilet floor.

Not surprisingly, we never made it in the USA. No hit records. No 'word on the street' buzz. No 'the next big thing from the UK' headlines. The whole thing just ground to a halt - gigs were cancelled, as word of our massive unreliability and supreme incompetence reached the clubs and colleges that we relied upon to keep us on the road.

The days of the staggering, swaggering British rock band rolling into town waving bottles of Jack Daniels were in the past. There was now a new breed of American band whose enormous tour bus always arrived on time, who carried briefcases and nurtured lucrative corporate sponsorships. They might have looked like rock and roll stars when they were on stage, but they were from a long tradition of showbusiness.

The record company stopped returning our calls and our credit cards were cancelled. We had no choice but to return home, our parents paying for the flights. Our equipment - battered and bruised by this stage, like us - is still in the stairwell of a small basement club in Rapid City, South Dakota, as far as I know.

VII

When we returned home, we all needed a few weeks to recuperate. Basically, we were broke, exhausted and humiliated. I slept in my old room at my parents' house till noon, never leaving the house. My Mum would cook me a meal and in the evenings we'd watch television together, as though none of this had ever happened.

One by one, the others left the band - not that it really existed anymore. Jon's parents sent him to some sort of clinic, where he was treated for his drink problem and general ill-health, eventually returning to work once again in his Dad's shop. There was talk of going back to college and pursuing a career in accountancy.

Gary disappeared soon after our return to the UK, re-surfacing years later as the manager of a Hard Rock Café in Singapore. Mickey and I decided to soldier on.

Drummers and bass players are easily replaced, we thought, especially as we were a 'name band'. The trouble is, we had nothing to offer to new recruits. There was no money, no gigs and no recording contract. Everyone had forgotten us, apart from a small hard core of loyal fans. The music industry had moved on and we were history.

After a few rehearsals with a succession of terrible bass players and drummers, Mickey decided to call it a day. He passed away a few years later, from pancreatic cancer. He'd been complaining about pains in his back for years and when he eventually went to a doctor and got the diagnosis, it was too late. His funeral made the local paper, under the headline 'Local music legend takes final bow'. It was on page 14, underneath an article about a dog show.

Although Gary, Mickey and Jon were gone, I kept the faith. And the band name. More fool me. For 40 years now, Pale Monarch has been the only constant in my life, as two divorces ensured that I lost what little wealth I had accumulated.

My Father passed away a few years ago. I'm sure that my continued use of the name he originated would have caused him great amusement, as well as confirming that his judgement of me was correct.

With a revolving door of temporary band members, it's been a steady dribble of gigs here and in parts of Europe, where for some reason the name Pale Monarch still means something. Or did. There have also been extended periods of inactivity and half-hearted reunions with whichever original members were available at the time.

Gigs have gradually become smaller and less frequent - support slots for other bands you thought had broken-up years ago, shabby provincial basement clubs, arts centres in converted gas works, festivals the size of village fetes, pubs of all shapes and sizes. It's called the Toilet Circuit, for good reason.

The occasional self-funded album has been released and disappeared without trace. Our old albums have been re-released, but we don't see any of the money as any rights we might have had were sold back to the record company years ago, as part-payment for the many advances we had squandered.

Inevitably perhaps, my lifestyle is not as healthy as I might have hoped after crawling back from America all those years ago. I've been off the drugs for some time now - most of them, anyway - but I still like a drink and smoke like a chimney.

I live in a mobile home with a girl 25 years younger than me, who also likes a drink and a smoke. We met in a pub after a gig a year or so ago: she came home with me and has never left. She keeps an eye on me, for which I'm very grateful.

I'm still a member of the gig economy, but these days most of my gigs involve manual labour - builder's labourer, van driver or warehouseman. Despite all this, fans - and we still have a few - seem to think that we're a proper band, that we do this full-time and make a reasonable living.

Perhaps they think we all live together in a house, like the old Monkees TV show, all running around at double-speed, playing wacky pranks on each other.

The band these days is me and three local guys, all a few years younger than me. Jon's nephew, Pete, is on guitar, a friend of his, Dave, is on bass and Steve Green, a long-term fan, plays drums. We play gigs at weekends - not every weekend - and sometimes manage to link a few gigs together, so we can pretend it's a tour. We play all the old songs and the audience still join in the chorus of Dirty Woman, like they always have done.

It's not all plain sailing. For example, the other day, I overheard the other three band members discussing how to replace me with a new singer. How did they think they could still call themselves Pale Monarch without me, the only original member?

Despite this, we've enjoyed a few highlights in recent years, so maybe there's a second coming in the offing. Not 'American Tour' or 'Top of the Pops' highlights, it's true, but events like the Butlins Festival of 70s Rock are what keep me going.

It's not all that glamorous, I have to admit. There is no dressing room or free drinks, and you have to queue for over-priced lager and burgers with the rest of the punters. But there's always a large, appreciative audience and they treat us with respect. And for me, that makes it all worthwhile.

After our set at this year's Butlins, I met a group of ladies from Matlock, cackling away over their Prosecco and Gin, passing around pictures of their Grandchildren on their phones. I haven't seen my own Grandkids for years - or my kids, come to that - but I joined these lovely ladies at their table and managed to fake an interest in theirs.

I got talking to the woman next to me - red haired, short denim skirt, faded tattoos, dirty laugh - and one thing led to another, as things tend to do. The band took the mick, saying she was - how can I put it politely - a little on the large side. But I've put a fair few pounds on myself over the years, so who am I to judge?

Later that evening, there was a slightly undignified scene in her chalet, which I prefer not to dwell on. The band were right about her size, but I persevered, did what needed to be done, and ended up climbing out of the bedroom window while she was in the loo. Well, I do still have some standards after all these years.

And I kept her rather large knickers in my pocket, as a souvenir for the lads. A real rock and roll moment, I think you'll agree, and typical of the classy way I have conducted myself over the years. It's what Pale Monarch stood for and I think that my Father would have been proud.

VIII

So there you have it, that's my life as a rock star. Such as it was.

I'm still lying here on my back, drifting in and out of consciousness, looking up at a blur of worried faces. I feel strangely at peace. If this is the end, so be it - it's been a blast.

People are slapping my face. Splashing water on to me. Shouting at me.

'Wake up Max, you drunken old bastard. We're on stage in ten minutes.'

THE BUSINESS LUNCH

I

1982

'Welcome to Grimsby', says the taxi driver cheerily and without any obvious irony, as he pulls up outside the apparently derelict building by the docks.

It's another cold, grey day in the fish capital of Thatcher's Britain. Strong wind and rain are lashing in vertically from the sea. A lone seagull hovers overhead, squawking angrily as it prepares to loosen its bowels. There is an overpowering smell of rotting seafood and diesel oil, a combination that fills the many puddles on the road.

Jane Hall surveys the cobbled and rutted street and the deserted industrial landscape that surrounds her - abandoned Victorian warehouses to one side, empty docks to the other - and reminds herself why she's here. This is her first proper assignment, after a year as a management trainee at the head office of the Empire and Colonial Food Group (EFG) – a year spent mainly filing and photocopying documents in the group marketing department. It's the chance to make a name for herself - Jane is fiercely ambitious and does not intend to let anyone or anything stand in her way.

It's a hell of a place to start. Her new employer, EFG Seafoods, is one of the least-profitable businesses in the entire group, with a track record of declining sales and retail distribution, appalling advertising and products of wartime quality. Hall's new role was widely discussed amongst her fellow trainees as being the least attractive placement option by some distance and she wonders whether her status as the only female in the group of eight had anything to do with her posting.

Now in her early twenties, Jane had been a force to be reckoned with at Oxford Girls School, where she was a prefect and captain of the Hockey team. At Cambridge, she had excelled in her chosen subjects of economics and finance, and her striking good looks (which spoke more of health than beauty) had ensured an active social and love life.

Having chosen the world of business, her ambition and motivation is to go all the way to the top - and she is prepared to do whatever it takes, starting today.

Product Manager for the Fishworthy brand of processed fish and simulated potato ready meals may not have been the most promising start, but she was determined to make it work. Even by the standards of EFG, this is a product range of such low quality that most of its sales are in the foodservice sector, for consumption (it was widely assumed) in cost-driven institutions catering for people with no choice in the matter - care homes, mental institutions, the more secure sort of prison, motorway service stations, for example.

Time to think positive, she thinks, inhaling deeply as she opens the door to a mild gale, stepping into a particularly deep and malodorous puddle. 'You can't beat the good old British seaside, can you?' she remarks to the driver, in what she hopes is a humorous tone.

'I prefer Torremolinos myself,' he replies, taking her bags from the boot and dumping them in a rancid pool of reeking liquid, before jerking a thumb at one of the less abandoned buildings. 'The offices are over there.'

Jane lugs her bags to the front and finds what might once have been an impressive front door, with a sign next to it: 'EFG Seafoods. Gutting Shed and Marketing Department'. After she has pressed the buzzer repeatedly, the door finally creaks open of its own accord.

There is no reception area and Jane enters a large room full of women standing at a conveyor belt of industrial revolution vintage whilst disembowelling fish. The stench and noise are overpowering. Pop music is being played through a tinny speaker system but is almost drowned out by the volume of the women talking to each other and the creaking protestations of the antiquated machinery.

Swallowing her bile, Hall speaks to the nearest woman. 'Good morning. My name's Jane Hall and I'm here to see Richard Price-Brown.'

She is greeted by a cacophony of laughter and rude remarks, many of them poking fun at her 'la-di-da' accent and others asking what Lady Bloody Di was doing here. One of them points at an office in the furthermost, dankest, part of the building, marked 'Marketing'.

Hall walks towards it, finding two elderly men in brown overalls standing at a bench, packing some sort of fish by-product slowly into boxes. Cigarettes hang from their lips, with ash dropping into the boxes. They look up at Jane, laugh mysteriously through their toothless mouths, and carry on. Jane opens the door and walks in.

II

The man Jane is to meet - Richard Price-Brown - is Marketing Manager at Empire Seafoods and will be her boss. He too is new to Grimsby, having joined last month from EFG Fats, the UK subsidiary of the Argentinian Lard Company, a distant part of the Empire and Colonial Foods Group.

It was not entirely a co-incidence that his Father was Group Finance Director, but he had been assured that he had been given the job entirely on his own merits. His third-class degree in Theology fell short of EFG's usual requirements, but as he had not been required to complete an application form, or to attend an interview, this did not seem to matter.

His first six months at EGF Fats had been spent on assignment with the sales team and had consisted mainly of getting lost in his company car (a clapped-out Morris Marina), arriving late for customer meetings, and vomiting after drinking too much at sales conferences. However, he had then spent a glorious, God-like, period as Junior Product Manager, responsible for the development, triumphant launch and subsequent withdrawal from the market of CanDoo.

It could all have been so different, reflected Price-Brown. Yes, there were problems – CanDoos's appearance, aroma, palatability, profitability and taste all left a lot to be desired - but these could probably have been resolved over time. After all, this was a product at the leading-edge of innovation - the world's first non-dairy cheese, in an aerosol can.

Consider the ingredients - a unique combination of lard crust, processed stomach lining, reconstituted whey and intestinal mucus. Once a cocktail of food additives had been added, the taste was tangy and addictive.

Yet the total cost was next to nothing and the ingredients would otherwise have been treated by the company as effluent and discharged under cover of darkness into the nearest watercourse.

Once the factory had worked its magic, CanDoo offered children an unhealthy and life-limiting treat, squirted at high volume and with ozone-damaging potential from an aerosol can, at a surprisingly low price. The product surely embodied everything EFG stood for, he had thought proudly.

No product had been quite so controversial in research, gaining the first-ever negative score from the UK Food Panel, and rousing many consumers to anger, vomiting and in one case extreme violence, exacted upon the unfortunate figure of Price-Brown, left cowering in the corner of a consumer group in Dudley.

But what did consumers know? As Henry Ford once said, 'If I'd given my customers what they asked for, I'd have built a faster horse'. And Richard was reasonably confident that, unlike EFGs meat pie range, CanDoo had absolutely no equine content.

After his enforced departure from EFG Fats, Price-Brown had enjoyed a brief nine-month period of rest, relaxation, quiet desperation and increasingly suicidal tendencies.

Fortunately, his Father had been able to find him another role within EFG and, armed with a long-held deep commitment to processed economy-grade fish, acquired the night before the interview, he had been offered the Marketing Manager's job at EFG Seafoods.

Conveniently located just 350 miles from his home, he would now be renting a squalid flat over a chip shop and visiting his family - who had refused to move to Grimsby - at weekends.

At the age of 26, Price-Brown was already balding and, despite his many inadequacies, assumed the air of effortless superiority, omniscience and pomposity normally found in a much older man. He was determined to make a success of his new role and to build a successful career within the food industry, starting at EFG Seafoods. He would ensure that no-one stood in his way, least of all some fast-track blue-stocking like Jane Brown.

III

As Jane enters the office, Price-Brown rises to his feet and introduces himself.

'Hello, I'm Richard Price-Brown. Welcome to Grimsby', the words fully-loaded with intentional irony. 'Are you ready to eat? If so, and given the time of day, please allow me to introduce you to the joys of lunch at EFG Seafoods. It will have to be the canteen, I'm afraid.'

He leads Jane back to the other side of the Gutting Hall, through some filthy see-through plastic swing doors, and along a corridor with noticeboards on one side and doors to lavatories on the other. As they reach the canteen, they are met with the steamy aroma of over-cooked food and the overwhelming noise of shouted conversations, clanking cutlery and clattering plates. Jane finds it depressing beyond words and makes a note to bring her own sandwiches in future.

'I'll sort out payment, seeing as you're new,' offers Price-Brown, thrusting a tray at Jane. 'My advice is not to look too closely at the food and to avoid the soup at all costs. If you went to public school, like me, there's nothing to worry about, but it does take some people a while to acclimatise. If you need to throw up, please be discreet - it reflects badly on the marketing department. But to look on the bright side, all the food here is supplied by EFG, so it's a great opportunity to sample what the Group has to offer.'

Jane has no idea what food is scooped onto her plate - she just takes what she's given, while the counter staff shout unintelligibly at her.
She sits down with Price-Brown and two people she has never met before, but before she can introduce herself, they all dive into their food with

apparent enthusiasm. Price-Brown has a plate completely covered in glutinous brown gravy, from which various irregular shapes protrude, while the two strangers have today's special - a heap of barely-cooked chips, blackened fried fish and a steaming pile of lurid green mushy peas. Jane can barely bring herself to look at the mysterious pool of slop on her plate and eats as little of it as she thinks she can get away with. They all drink water from heavily-stained malodorous plastic beakers.

As soon as they've finished, Price-Brown rises from his seat, mumbling 'Ah well, no peace for the wicked' as he strides for the door. Jane follows him, if only to get out of the canteen.

'So that's the Empire Seafoods canteen,' he says. 'All the EFG products are pretty damn good, as you've just found out, but I have to admit that overall, it was not a lunch to remember. I'm sure there will be many more business lunches for both of us in the years to come. All of them a lot better than that one. In fact, I'm banking on it.'

Me too, thinks Jane.

IV

The next morning, Jane attends the monthly marketing and sales meeting, chaired by Price-Brown in the absence of Peter Young, the sales and marketing director, who was on one of his monthly trips to London to 'see the agency'.

It was widely assumed that Young's day with the advertising agency involved little more than a lengthy lunch, during which he was expertly wined, dined and massaged by the agency team, before being sent by cab to King's Cross, bloated and drunk, to fall asleep on the train back to Grimsby. It was lunches like these that kept the agency on its toes and ensured effective use of the multi-million pound EFG Seafoods advertising budget, he told himself and anyone who would listen. No-one believed him.

Jane has made a great effort to be nondescript and has tied her hair in a bun, worn no make-up and chosen her dullest clothes - a navy jacket, navy calf-length skirt and flat shoes. Despite this, as she enters the meeting room she is greeted with a barrage of 'humorous' comments, ranging from 'hello lads, the stripper's arrived' to 'don't fancy yours much, Jim'. To a man - and they are all men - the assembled EFG Seafoods sales team looks Jane up and down lecherously as Price-Brown makes the introductions.

The first item on the agenda is to ask each member of the sales team - an unwieldy bureaucracy of national account managers, regional sales managers and field sales representatives - for their feedback on the performance of Fishworthy. A middle-aged manager, sweat staining the armpits of his cheap poly-cotton shirt, is addressing the meeting in an aggressive midlands accent.

'And this bloody 'Scampi with Free Garlic Butter' idea is complete nonsense, as well. My customers want multi-pack value deals, not this marketing crap. Who eats garlic outside of London? This won't get me full Presto red-dot support, let alone a South Midlands Co-Op 'Value Bonanza' shelf-strip price deal.'

He sits down self-righteously to a mutter of approval from his sales colleagues, most of whom have been too busy filling in expense forms to pay attention. However, salespeople enjoy nothing better than kicking a marketing person when they're down, so a few others join in.

'And what about this aerosol fish paste product?' asks a ginger-haired man with a strong Scottish accent. 'It might have worked for cheese, but if you think I'm showing that to the buyer at William Jackson, you've got another bloody think coming. Fishy Whippy, my arse.'

Price-Brown took the chair and spoke in his usual languid manner. 'Some very interesting points there, Gentlemen. Thank you all so much. I'd love to respond, but this is all very much Jane's baby, and I'm sure she'll be able to provide you with detailed answers. Jane?'

He leans back in his chair, satisfied that the buck has been passed in its entirety, and puts his hands behind his head in eager anticipation of some sport.

Jane has prepared a detailed presentation, including a strategy review, a summary of the latest retail audit data, and a proposed plan for the rest of the year. She was up till late completing it and her acetate slides sit quivering in a towering stack, next to the overhead projector. However, she hadn't anticipated quite so much criticism directed at things which had been decided before she joined.

'Perhaps the best way for me to deal with those issues is to take you through my brand review and...'

She is interrupted with a barrage of comments, all of which seem to suggest that the last thing any of them want is another bloody marketing presentation, which should instead be rolled up, greased and inserted where the sun doesn't shine. The smell of cheap aftershave, body odour and bad breath is almost overpowering, as is the sense of a pack of wild animals closing in for the kill.

Price-Brown turns to a rather shaken Jane, 'Well Jane, it rather looks as though the entire sales team has some serious concerns with your brand. I for one am in total agreement and I think they deserve a proper response.' Once again, he sat back in his chair, awaiting her public humiliation.

'Thank you, Richard,' responds Jane, picking herself up bravely, as though recovering from a hard blow with a hockey stick in a tough match against Malvern College.

'I'll cut to the chase, then. I have reviewed the brand plans - which were excellent, by the way, and were, I note, signed-off by none other than your good self, Richard.' She pauses for effect and is pleased to see some nods and smiles around the table.

'But excellent as they were, I felt that there was way too much focus on advertising and new product development, and nowhere near enough spend on sales and trade support, which as we all know, is where anything that matters happens.'

There is a rumble of agreement from around the room and Jane carries on.

'Accordingly, I am recommending diverting most of the brand's budget to trade support activity, to be used at the discretion of each member of the sales team. I'll be sending out plans to each of you later this week.'

She sits down to a round of applause. Her shameless improvisation and outright lies mean that she now has the sales team in the palm of her hand. Not an entirely pleasant idea, she thinks, but it's all part of her strategy.

At the other end of the table, she can see that Price-Brown is furious at her successful turning of the tables. He was clearly not to be trusted and she would ensure that he wouldn't get away with anything like that again. There could only be one winner and it was going to be her.

Price-Brown is speaking. 'Now for our guest speaker. I've asked Dr Eric Watt, the EFG Group Research and Development director, along today to give us all an update on the amazing work that he and his team of mad scientists do to give our products their competitive edge. Over to you, Eric.'

Watt rises to his feet. In his late 50s, with a white coat and long, thinning white hair, he did indeed resemble a mad scientist. A Scot, he speaks with a soft, hypnotic lowland burr that draws the audience into his confidence.

'As you all know, EFG is legendary for its commitment to innovation.'

He pauses and looks around the room to a sea of blank faces, aware of no such thing, and continues.

'To achieve this, we in the R&D team work to three guiding principles: flexibility, creativity and transformation. All of this is intended to deliver the lowest acceptable product quality at the lowest possible cost. To help us to do this, we have developed a world-leading portfolio of new and better food additives, coupled with the use of low-cost raw materials not previously considered as food ingredients.'

'Let me give you a few examples' he continues, putting an acetate slide onto the overhead projector. 'I'm sure you'll agree that our Home Maid apple pies - that's them on the screen - are absolutely delicious. Yet they are the cheapest on the market, undercutting our nearest competitor by almost 20%. How do we do this? Well, most of the apple is in fact sliced potato, injected with artificial flavouring and soaked in sweeteners. No-one can tell the difference - and it means that at a stroke the food cost for this product is reduced by more than 50%.'

He changes to the next acetate slide, as some of the sales team make 'OK, we're now impressed' noises.

'Much the same applies to all our other fruit-based products, including our extra-fruity yogurts. Apples, bananas, peaches and pears? Maybe, but most of it will be potato. Real fruit is history, in terms of mass food production, Gentlemen. At the same time, all our potato-based products now use bleached vegetable waste - corn husks, sprout stalks, pea pods, that sort of thing - to add bulk and texture. And of course, to reduce costs. Best of all, the farmers even pay us to take it all away! Now that's what I call flexible. That's what I call creative!'

He pauses for applause and is duly rewarded. He now has the audience firmly on his side. This is all new to most of the sales team and one of them, an enthusiastic red-faced rep called Hewison, asks a question.

'This is absolutely brilliant, Dr Watt. But surely, all this has to be declared on the product labelling, doesn't it?'

Watt smiles. 'Good question. Fortunately for us, the law is an ass and as you'll see, that definitely applies to food labelling.'

'We can and do state 'vegetables' - not 'food waste', obviously - on our labels. Everyone loves veggies! Then, we break down ingredients which are too high in percentage terms, or too unattractive sounding, into a number of sub-ingredients and give them completely authentic Latin or scientific names, which we make up if necessary. And let's face it, when it's all set in small type in ten different languages, on the side of a small packet, no-one can read it anyway.'

As the laughter dies away, he carries on. 'Here's another example of flexibility. All our Meatworthy meat products - and there are at least 30 in the range - share exactly the same basic ingredient. This is a slurry manufactured from cheap food waste - sorry, vegetables - and mechanically-recovered meat - that's the stuff we extract by high pressure hose from carcasses after all the good stuff has been used. This slurry accounts for 95% of the total volume of each product and then we just add a little of the headline ingredient - beef, say - plus the legal maximum of artificial flavourings. Once even the smallest amount of beef has been added, we are allowed to call the product itself Beef Stew, or whatever. And of course, absolutely any part of a cow can be called Beef. And I do mean any part.'

'But enough of cows. We're in Grimsby today, so let's talk fish. Obviously, this business is not located in Grimsby because it's a fishing port - that would be absurd. No, we're here because property and labour are cheap. Like most products in any category, nearly all our fish these days comes from China, where it is mass-produced in enormous commercial lagoons, once famous for their pollutants, poisons and raw sewage - until our PR and legal people quietened things down, that is. This has two massive advantages for us: it's ridiculously cheap, obviously, and the fish comes to us as large generic frozen blocks, which we can then convert to whatever variety of fish-based product we want. And because we do that here, in Grimsby, we are able to state that the UK is the country of origin. Like I told you - the law's an ass.'

At this juncture, the meeting is interrupted, as were so many in those days, by a large clanking tea trolley, pushed by two cackling crones with strong local accents.

As far as the tea ladies are concerned, the meeting exists only so that all present can drink weak tea from brown cups and saucers. Once orders have been taken and the tea has been distributed, Watt continues.

'Finally, I'd like to talk about transformation. As I told you earlier, we are able to transform raw ingredients that would otherwise be completely inedible - like vegetable stalks, food waste or animal parts - into products that people, particularly the lower socio-economic orders, find absolutely delicious. And even better, addictive. That's the EFG way.'

'All this you may already know, but you may be surprised to learn that we're now working on a new and rather exciting development - a project to extract the protein from animal and human excrement and use it in our products.'

Another pause, while the sales team takes in the magnitude of this development. 'New and rather exciting' is one way to put it. There are others, it turns out: 'Holy Shit', for example.

'This project is quite far advanced now and we hope to have some news - related initially to our Cornish Pasty 'protein-enriched' product range - very soon. Of course, we've been using urine for some years - it adds a refreshing sparkle and essential vitamins to adult health drinks and children's juices alike. And luckily for us, there is always a steady flow to hand, at little or no cost.'

Watt pauses to allow the sales team to joke about excrement and urine, which they do with enthusiasm and predictability, before continuing.

'Anyway, it has been a pleasure meeting you all today. I hope I have shown you what we in R&D are doing to keep costs low, our products appealing and our business profitable. And as a member of the senior management team, can I also say that I'm particularly delighted to see our new recruit - a lady at that - making such a strong impression. It certainly looks like she's going to keep you on your toes, Richard.'

The meeting closed, Price-Brown strides grim-faced from the room, ignoring Jane. It was clear that they were now sworn enemies, which suited Jane fine. *It's him or me.* She decides to speak with Watt as he packs his briefcase.

'Thank you for your presentation, Dr Watt. I really enjoyed it, but I couldn't help noticing that the company seems to use an awful lot of food additives. Aren't they dangerous?'

Watt laughs. 'Yes, guilty as charged - we're the single largest user of food additives in Europe. How else could we make our products taste so good? I mean, look at what they're made of. But I can assure you that they are completely harmless to the consumer - the amount of any one additive in a single serving is miniscule.' Watt pauses, looking thoughtful.

'However, in their concentrated form - as they are delivered to us and stored in the warehouse - they are extremely powerful and can be poisonous in surprisingly small volumes. For example, just a few drops of Mexedrine can kill - and as it's a clear liquid with no aroma or flavour, we have to be extremely vigilant.'

Jane thanks him, shakes his hand and leaves. She didn't want to miss her next appointment - a tour of the factory and warehouse by the factory manager, John Nichol. When she'd met him earlier, she knew he would be putty in her hands and now, thanks to Watt, she knew exactly how she could make use of him. She loosens a few buttons on her blouse and reaches into her handbag for some lipstick. Surprisingly small volumes, indeed.

V

London, 1986
'It looks like the hanging gardens of Babylon,' says Jane, as she and Richard climb out of their taxi.

The Riverside Terrace, London's most expensive restaurant, is located on a series of multi-level platforms suspended above the Thames, between Vauxhall and Lambeth bridges.

The chef-patron, Albert Raymond, is proud of his three Michelin stars and has left nothing to chance. CCTV cameras have spotted their taxi slowing down and a red carpet has already been unfurled.

They are greeted at the door by the Maitre D', who leads them through the opulent surroundings of the reception area, past a row of grim, unsmiling waiting staff, to their table overlooking the Thames. Jane can't help noticing the glass floor, beneath which the river swirls menacingly.

Their guests are already seated. Simon Hogg is Editor of Grocery Times, the UK's most important trade publication, and he is joined by a female colleague, who is introduced as Kasia Lateef. As his surname suggests, Hogg is pink and plump, while Kasia is much younger and, Jane guesses, very junior - probably a trainee that Hogg is trying to impress.

Richard explains that as he has recently been promoted to Sales & Marketing Director, and Jane to Marketing Manager, they welcome the opportunity of meeting such pre-eminent journalists as Simon and Kasia, in order to provide an updated briefing on EFG Seafoods. As he is quick to point out, EFG is brand leader in the sub-economy sector of the ready-to-eat fish market.

They are particularly keen, he says, to correct the erroneous impression some journalists and retailers have of EFG Seafoods as a third-rate manufacturer of sub-standard economy food products. Asian lagoon-farmed fish composite was barely radioactive these days, and in some cases was hardly infected with lice or bacteria at all – or at least, certainly not to the extent that it once was.

The company was proud to provide economical and filling meal solutions for many hard-working families, he says, with apparent sincerity. The range and quality of these were continually improving as the result of the legendary innovation, and extensive arsenal of new and better food additives, for which EFG Seafoods was justifiably famous.

Simon Hogg nods wisely, aware that little more was expected of him.

The implicit understanding was that this lunch was simply an excuse to be wined and dined at London's most expensive - and otherwise unaffordable - restaurant, at someone else's expense. Certain favours were expected in return.

Hence, business would not be discussed beyond Price-Brown's preamble. From now on, the Grocery Times would look more favourably on press releases sent to it by EFG Seafoods PR agency, Pragmatic PR, whose director, Rosalyn Parker, had worked long and hard to set up this lunch.

Jane sips her champagne, looks at the view and reflects on the chain of events that has brought her to this temple of gastronomy, the polar opposite of everything that EFG Seafoods and its Grimsby location stand for.

On the one hand, it goes without saying that the Riverside Terrace is so much better than the canteen at Grimsby: this really is a proper Business Lunch, and one that will give her bragging rights with her friends for some time. On the other hand, there was just about everything else - the company, its offices, its products and the people she has to work with, especially the odious Price-Brown.

In fact, it turns out that having EFG Seafoods on your CV is practically career suicide. Goodness knows she'd tried hard enough to get another job. This means that promotion within the EFG Group is now her only career option.

However, despite her recent elevation to marketing manager, little had changed. She still had to work for Price-Brown, who did everything he could to undermine her and to promote his own interests to the detriment of hers. Her performance reviews were poor, her successes became his, while his failings - and there were many - became hers. If she was to progress her career, it would have to be at the expense of his.

Even at this lunch, he had made it clear who was in charge and had monopolised Hogg, leaving Jane to talk to Kasia, who seemed a little intimidated by the whole experience and had very little to say for herself.

Jane tried again: 'I'm going for the Menu Superbe, how about you, Kasia?'

'Yes, me too. It costs more than I earn in a week, so I'm going to make the most of it. For that price, I could probably buy a lifetime's supply of Fishworthy products, I should think. Not that I'd want to – after all, you wouldn't actually live for very long eating all that junk, would you.'

Kasia might be a little over-awed, and indeed somewhat unsophisticated and lacking in dress sense, thinks Jane. But she's quite sharp and will have to be watched. Jane decides to avoid rising to Kasia's criticism and to keep conversation as bland as possible.

'Yes - this is definitely what I would call premium pricing. Probably super-premium. I'm sure we can learn a lot from it.'

'But I don't suppose they use shit fish and multiple food additives here, do they? I'd love to know more about all that - is it true that the fish you buy is banned from human consumption in its country of origin?'

Jane again ignores Kasia's comments and is rescued by the arrival of the *amuse bouche* - minute slivers of deliciousness, probably conjured up from lark's tongues and angel's breath.

A five-course menu follows: pan-fried Foie Gras; grilled sea bass, in an apricot sauce; Challandais Duck with raspberries and blueberries, served at the table, the crisply-cooked legs arriving separately. Quince and apple sorbet follows; and a cheese trolley you could inhale from the other side of the room.

Mouthful after mouthful of superb food and none of it from a poisonous Asiatic lagoon, thinks Jane. This is my way of life now and no-one is going to get in my way, least of all that useless, conniving shit, Richard Price-Brown.

Price-Brown is busy savouring the wine, a 1992 Mouton Rothschild Pauillac, giving Hogg the benefit of his limited knowledge on the subject.

Even the cheapest bottles are priced at more than any sane person would pay for an entire case of perfectly decent wine, he thinks, which is precisely what makes it so great. However, he has previous form with wine-related disasters and now takes great care when in company.

Take the Louis Quatorze dining-room incident. Price-Brown winces as he recalls the private customer dinner at a stately home he had attended as a management trainee. After a huge swig, his mouth still full, he had sprayed most of the table with a spume of red wine whilst guffawing drunkenly. The white lace blouse of the client's wife sitting opposite him had been ruined. This has kept him awake at night on many occasions - and it is not the only such episode.

He couldn't afford any more humiliations and embarrassments if he was to achieve his career goals. He was already one of the youngest sales and marketing directors in the UK and intended to become managing director within three years. Nothing and no-one must stand in his way, certainly not Jane Hall, who was far too smart for her own good.

As the sun sets, the liqueur trolley is wheeled to their table by its ancient guardian, clanking across the restaurant towards them, row upon row of expensive bottles and yellowing labels awaiting their attention. By now, they are all in a stupefied haze of excess: time has telescoped and has little meaning.

Hogg considers at length the relative merits of a 10-year-old Chateau de Lacquy VSOP Armagnac and a Rémy Martin XO Cognac, while Price-Brown excuses himself and is escorted to the toilets by one of the ever-attentive waiting staff.

This is Jane's moment. Removing something from her handbag under the table, she leans across to talk to Hogg, whose Cognac now being poured with great ceremony. While he peers drunkenly down her blouse, she is able to tilt the small phial in her hand into Price-Brown's wine glass. A few drops are all that's needed.

Kasia, who does not drink, looks on impassively.

V1

London, 2016
Cassie Blackburn sips her coffee and looks out of her office window.

From the 20th floor, London spreads out before her, the river snaking across the city. On one side, she can see the Shard, on the other, the increasingly futuristic buildings of the City. In the distance, Canary Wharf is shrouded in mist. Through the glass walls of her office, she can see her team hard at work in their cubicles. Life is good for a poor girl from an immigrant family.

Or it was, until she realised her job was under threat.

The drip-feed of comments and jokes about her age told their own story and at the age of 52, Cassie knew that she was now considered to be too old for her job as City Editor at the Daily Post. All the Editor needed was an excuse.

There would be a good pay-off, of course. And much as she hated to admit it, it would be much too good to turn down. She already hated herself for not taking the paper to court for ageism. She'd overcome racism and sexism in her career - and more recently, a few jokes about her size, too. Now this.

That's why this story is so important to her. If she can pull it off, anything is possible. Her Editor would certainly sit up and pay attention, but so would other Editors, in larger and better papers than the Daily Post. A devastating exposé of the business practices of one of the world's largest food businesses, it would propel her into another league altogether.

She reviews the email she is sending to her Editor. She has finally managed to arrange lunch with the Group CEO of the business she has been investigating and needs to protect herself and the paper, given the legal implications of her investigation.

Scrolling down, she starts to read.

From: Cassie Blackburn
To: Sandra Cook
cc. Douglas Andrews, Ray Marshall, Mike Smithers
Subject: Empire & Colonial Food Group

I wanted to let you know that I am meeting the Group CEO of the Empire & Colonial Food Group (now known as EFG) for lunch tomorrow.

Our investigations have uncovered a culture and history of illegal and immoral business practices at this group of food companies, which are directly related to their extraordinary profitability. I intend to confront the CEO with our findings and so wanted to ensure that you are all fully-briefed, from an editorial and legal standpoint.

As you are no doubt aware, EFG is one the world's largest consumer packaged food and beverage manufacturers, with net sales of $18bn dollars and 45,000 employees in more than 40 countries. It was formed as the result of a series of acquisitions and mergers by the former Empire & Colonial Food Group, following its IPO in 2005.

Unlike its competitors, EFG does not boast of its high quality, great-tasting and nutritional products, or its mission of sustainability. Instead, it boasts that consumers 'don't want to save the planet, they want to save money' and 'don't want the best food, they want the cheapest food'.

The issues I want to address are these: what is the true cost of that cheap food? What shortcuts has EFG taken to provide it? And what are the legal and ethical implications?

The roots of this can be traced back to the original Empire & Global Food Group. Even fifty years ago, it was a large food production, manufacturing and distribution group in its own right, based in the UK but operating in most of the World.

Its strength was in its extensive but largely unknown mastery of vertical integration. As well as factories and shops, it owned abattoirs, cattle ranches, cold stores, distribution centres, ships, docks, insurance companies, vehicle fleets, companies, warehouses - not to mention a shadowy network of service businesses, from law firms to printworks.

Its overseas land holding was four times the size of Britain - cattle, pigs, sheep, tea and coffee plantations, you name it. There are even rumours that in some of the more remote locations it is still run almost entirely by slave labour.

Not surprisingly, given its name, the roots of EFG were in the British Empire and the British Commonwealth, and more specifically, in the ruthless exploitation of non-British countries for profit. Most of the business is shrouded in secrecy, not least because up until the IPO in 2005, the business was in the private hands of the sinister Walker family, ancestors of the rapacious Mancunian Grocers who started the business in the 19th century.

The CEO up to the IPO was a particularly evil family member called Daniel Walker, who took the Group's business practices to new and quite extraordinary extremes, even for EFG. Walker - now Sir Daniel – has become Chairman and from EFG's Head Office, a grim Victorian building on the South Bank of the Thames, he continues to direct the vast and impenetrable EFG operation, consisting of many hundreds of interlocking companies, offshore trusts and tax dodges.

In summary, EFG was a masterpiece of vertical integration, entrepreneurial flair, cruelty and greed - and probably still is. Things may even have got worse, as the Group has expanded into markets with little regulation, who welcome the investment.

Our research suggests that this complex organisation and its culture of secrecy has allowed the company to sidestep just about every food production and employment law there is, globally.

As a result, its costs are incredibly low, its use of food additives extremely high and the exact nature of what is used to make its products unknown - for example, hitherto-unused animal parts, food waste and infected or polluted raw materials. There are even rumours of new technology that extracts protein from human excrement and uses it for food production.

There is little doubt that the company's huge profits have been made as the direct result of these practices and I intend to confront the recently appointed CEO, Jane Hall, with this when I meet her tomorrow.

I also have an extremely serious personal matter to raise with her, related to her own career progression, which is so sensitive that I have not yet added it to my notes or files. I will brief you personally when we next meet.

Cassie Blackburn
City Editor

VII

Jane Hall walks briskly across the restaurant, led by two waiting staff. Now in her mid-fifties, her appearance has changed little over the years, other than the added layer of sophistication that comes with the grooming and personal budgets available to the CEO of one of the largest food conglomerates in the world.

Her new role - she had been appointed the previous year - carries a salary in excess of a million pounds, all manner of benefits and stock options worth many millions. It had taken of lot of persuasion to get the Chairman, Sir Daniel Walker, to appoint her to the top job. In the end, a combination of sex - he had unusual tastes, she discovered - and the subtle suggestion of blackmail had been necessary.

After thirty years, she was finally one of the most powerful people in the global food industry - and certainly the most powerful woman. Her career goals had been achieved and, as always, she would do whatever it took to defend her position.

At the far side of the restaurant, she is greeted by a smartly-dressed dark-haired woman, a little on the short and plump side, who stands up and holds out an elegant hand, gold bangles dangling from her light brown wrist.

'Cassie Blackburn. And you are Jane Hall, of course. How lovely to meet you at last.'

Jane returns the greeting, noting how confident and self-assured this woman is. Not that it would make any difference - Jane had dealt with many journalists in her time and none of them had ever left a meeting knowing any more than Jane wanted them to. She had also been to many impressive restaurants, but she had to admit that this one was probably up there with the best.

Opened the previous month amidst an expensive but focused launch campaign, ArtHäus was much more than just a restaurant. In fact, it was five restaurants, four bars and a tea-room, all located within a beautiful 18th century townhouse in Belgravia.

Michelin-starred food was its main claim to fame, but art, fashion and music were all featured in various ways. Cassie had been told that just last night, Justin Bieber had performed an impromptu solo concert in one of the bars, seated at the grand piano. Some of Damien Hurst's work was on show in the men's washroom. It was that kind of place.

The interior looks as though it might have been designed by a rap star with an unlimited budget, unexpectedly good taste and expert assistance. The wallpaper, carpets, fabrics and furnishings are exquisite, to the smallest detail. Words like *lavish, opulent, stunning* and *completely over-the-top* are regularly used by restaurant reviewers, as well as by the customers, typically the international super-rich, A-list celebrities and the highest-earning Premier League footballers.

Taking a sip of her champagne, Jane turns to Cassie. 'So, Cassie. Why did you want to meet me - and why here, of all places, when I'd have been equally delighted to tell you what a fantastic business EFG is over a coffee in Starbucks.'

'All will be revealed, Jane. But first, shall we order? I don't know about you, but I'm famished. And the food is supposed to be rather good here, what with the Michelin stars and all.'

They manage some small talk over the food and wine. 'This is exceptional,' says Cassie. 'Perhaps you now understand why I brought you here. But before we get down to business, would you please excuse me while I powder my nose?'

Upon her return, Cassie sits down and leans forward. 'Shall I get straight to the point, Jane? I've gathered that you're the sort of person who prefers plain speaking.'

Jane nods and smiles encouragingly.

'EFG has been returning some impressive margins for a few years now,' begins Cassie. 'Margins previously unheard of in the food and beverage industry. And every year, they improve still further.'

Jane shrugs. After all, what else would you expect with her in charge?

Cassie continues. 'I asked myself how this could be possible, given the lack of investment by EFG over the years. Our research tells us that the main reason the company has such high margins is because it has consistently circumvented many global food production and employment standards and legislation. As a result of this, food costs are incredibly low, the use of food additives is amazingly high and the list of bizarre ingredients mentioned to us includes unknown animal parts, all manner of food waste and even human excrement.'

She pauses, allowing Jane to look surprised, and resumes.

'There can be little doubt that the company's huge profits are the result of extensive illegal and immoral practices, which you as Group CEO must be aware of.'

Jane looks impassive and speaks quietly, but with menace.

'That's all complete nonsense, Cassie, as you must know very well. There's no proof for any of your lies and I can assure you that if you dare to print any of them, we will sue your employer - and you, personally - to the full extent of the law and beyond. And I'll personally make sure that you never work in the media again.'

Cassie smiles. 'That's such a strong response that I can only assume everything I have said is correct, Jane. In fact, I raised some of these concerns with you when we last met, some years ago, so it's not as if anything I'm saying is new. You really don't remember me, do you?'

'I'm very sorry, Cassie, but I'm afraid I don't recall meeting you. You must be particularly unmemorable - some people are just more insignificant than others. You must be one of them.'

'Yes Jane, you were just as charming then, as I recall,' smiles Cassie. 'I could see what you were thinking - an unsophisticated little Asian girl, who didn't go to private school and Cambridge like you. But I can forgive your memory lapse – after all, it was back in the late 80s.'

'In that case, it's hardly surprising I don't recognise you, Cassie - we've probably both changed a little over the past 25 years. In my case, for the better. But please, do tell me more - I'm rather enjoying this little trip down memory lane.'

'We had lunch at the Riverside Terrace, back when it was *the* place in town. It was 1986 and we were both young and starting our careers. The Riverside Terrace was like another world to me then - and I think even you were a little impressed. I was with my boss, the editor of Grocery Times, and you were marketing manager at EFG Seafoods, with your boss, Richard Price-Brown. A lunch to remember - or at least, it was for me.'

Cassie takes a sip of her wine and continues.

'You knew me as Kasia Lateef back then, but I've always been known as Cassie and took my husband's name when we married a few years later. I was just a trainee reporter on a trade title back then, but I worked hard and here I am. The UK's leading female financial journalist – and I'm on *your* case, Jane. I'm afraid you seem to have rather under-estimated me.'

Cassie is getting a little worked up now and pauses for another sip of wine before she carries on. She doesn't want this to be too much of a tirade. Stay professional, she tells herself. She sips, breathes deeply, and continues.

'I haven't forgotten how that boss of yours - Price-Brown - died a few days after that lunch. The official announcement said that it was a heart attack, but they couldn't really be sure. That was a hell of a shock to me, as I'd had my bottom unexpectedly fondled by him at the Riverside just a few days before he died - but perhaps you weren't so surprised. I can't be certain, but I'm pretty sure I saw you drop something into his drink. I was young and lacking in confidence then, so I didn't say anything at the time. A smart career move on your part, perhaps. Who can say? Maybe now it's time to put the record straight.'

'Don't be so ridiculous,' interjects Jane. 'You've got absolutely no proof that I did any such thing.'

'Haven't I? Anyway, that's why I booked this restaurant, Jane. To return the compliment. You and your boss took us to what was then London's most expensive restaurant, so I've brought you here. But back to the 80's. Our research has found that even then, EFG Seafoods - and the entire EFG group as whole - was the largest user of food additives in Europe.'

'So what,' says Jane. 'Food additives are perfectly legal.'

'That's true - many food additives are legal. But back then, there was very little legislation. Some food additives were positively lethal - a few drops of concentrated Mexedrine, for example, could kill someone. It had no aroma, no flavour and was completely undetectable. Is that what you used on Price-Brown, Jane? But how would you have got your hands on

155

some? Someone as junior as you were back then wouldn't have had access to something like that.'

Jane sits back expressionless, her arms folded. Cassie continues.

'And then it all clicked into place. We interviewed a few people who were in the EFG Seafoods sales team back then. They're retired now, but they've never forgotten that ambitious young product manager - how could they, you were the first woman manager they'd ever seen and you weren't exactly a shrinking violet. And they all knew about your affair with the factory manager, John Nichol. A rather unattractive married man, twenty years older than you, they told me, who was responsible for the company's entire stock of food additives.'

She pauses, before going in for the kill. 'The rest is fairly obvious - just join the dots, including Nichol's death from a suspected heart attack soon after your affair ended. I can't prove any of this, yet - but I can certainly make it all sound very suspicious. Not to mention damaging to your reputation, the company's stock price – and the millions of pounds worth of stock options that you're sitting on. It's what we journalists do.'

Cassie sits back, waiting for Jane to crack. Instead, Jane raises her voice a level and looks Cassie in the eye, smiling.

'You stupid bitch, Kasia. I know exactly who you are. As soon as you made the lunch appointment, I had you checked out - we have people at EFG that do that sort of thing. And of course I remember you - a poor little trainee without much to say for herself, with no dress sense, greasy hair and fat legs. You've changed a little since then, I'll grant you - apart from the fat legs - but maybe you're not quite as smart as you think you are.'

Jane pauses, savouring Cassie's surprise. And it was going to get even better, very soon.

'Tell me, Cassie, did your researchers tell you that we've improved our range of food additives since those days? They're still poisonous in very small doses, but so much more sophisticated. For example, we've got a new one that, if used incorrectly, causes an almost immediate total loss of memory. It acts a lot faster than Mexedrine, too - a fatal heart attack within a few hours, or so I'm told. And best of all, it dissolves in the bloodstream, making it completely undetectable.'

'It really is a beautiful thing, Cassie. Even if you know that you've taken it, you soon forget all about it - and everything else as well. Best of all, no-one else will ever be able to tell that you took it. Women of our age are a bit prone to heart attacks and so on, aren't we - especially if we're a little overweight, like you. That's probably what they'll say happened, I expect. Such a shame, you still had so much to offer, even at your age.'

Jane pauses, allowing Cassie, who is looking a little confused, to think it all through.

'Mind you, some men prefer older women,' she continues. 'Nichol's successor, for example. Since I took him under my wing, young Whitworth has been very helpful to me regarding access to these new food additives, I have to say.'

Cassie stares at Jane, unable to speak. She can feel her face flushing as Jane's smile broadens.

'By the way, Cassie, I meant to ask you something. How did you enjoy your wine? Was it to your liking? It wasn't really a good time to powder your nose, was it.'

Cassie gasps as she finally realises the full horror of the situation. She can feel sweat on her brow and an accelerated heartbeat.

Jane held her smile. 'You won't remember a thing about this lunch in the few hours you've got left, Cassie. And it turns out that I was never here, anyway - I had someone phone your office an hour ago to say that I had to cancel at the last minute. Something came up, you know how it is, Cassie. I'm so sorry to let you down. Perhaps we can re-schedule - or perhaps not, in the circumstances.'

'Even better, as the table was booked in your name, there is no record of me at all. The staff don't know who I am and just to make sure, I'm wearing a wig. So goodbye Cassie, or Kasia, whatever your name is. This really.was a memorable lunch – for me, anyway.'

Jane waves her gloved hand at Cassie as she leaves, walking smartly through the restaurant. Cassie watches her leave, already forgetting everything.

THE LAST MEMORIAL
A TRUE STORY

Canvey Island, 2014

'And it was there, where we camped as kids, that we scattered Lee's mortal remains.'

A visibly upset Chris Fenwick is pointing at Long Horse Island, a mound of mud in the creek between Canvey Island and Hadleigh. He is standing on a bench, arms aloft, addressing a crowd of more than one hundred people. Almost messianic. We surround him and listen in silence to his words, born to us by the powerful Essex wind.

We are here to commemorate the death twenty years ago of Lee Brilleaux, lead singer of Dr Feelgood, the legendary British rhythm and blues group, who died of lymphoma on April 7th, 1994, aged forty-one. Fenwick, boyhood friend of Brilleaux and the manager of Dr Feelgood for the past forty years, is our guide on a walking tour of Canvey Island, where Brilleaux and the band grew up.

Tonight, we will attend the Lee Brilleaux Memorial Concert, which will feature members of Dr Feelgood past and present, as well as musical associates and friends. Those close to Lee and the band will be in attendance. The event sold out many months ago.

The first such concert took place on May 10th, 1994, the date of Brilleaux's birthday and just a month after his death. A local gig, for local people, it has become an annual event, including the walk, attracting pilgrims from all over the world.

But after twenty years, today - May 9th, 2014 - will be the last Lee Brilleaux Memorial Concert.

Canvey Tales

Our walk to Long Horse Island began that morning at the Lobster Smack, an unexpectedly picturesque pub, with 400 years of history, sited beneath the sea wall at the west end of the Island.
Shell Haven, the oil terminal, faces us and Canvey Wick Nature Reserve, which almost became an oil terminal itself, is behind.

'We started our little adventure here, 40 years ago' says Chris Fenwick, addressing us in stentorian tones from a staircase on the seawall, his voice rising and falling with the wind.

This is the location of the photograph on the cover of the first Dr Feelgood album, Down by the Jetty, released in January 1975. A dishevelled and sleepy Brilleaux is seen, head slumped, with the band, early one morning, having returned from a gig in London.

We walk along and below the sea wall, passing rusting oil industry artefacts - jetties, pipelines, storage tanks and terminals. Close by, the battered relics of a faded seaside resort are hard to avoid - funfairs, amusement arcades and caravan parks.

The procession lengthens the further we walk, past Dead Man's Point, Thorney Bay and the Labworth Café. This iconic grade 2 listed building, built in 1932 by Ove Larup from reinforced concrete to resemble the bridge of the Queen Mary, looks out to sea from its perch on the sea wall.

Fenwick's walking and story-telling set a cracking pace and if you can keep up, the tales keep coming. Bare-knuckle boxing, the importation of eels, friends of Lee with names like Dennis the Dog, Len the Hat and Colin the Socialist. Canvey Tales.

Canvey Island refuses to be typecast. A mudflat in the Thames Estuary, populated by the urban working class, it is also one of the most bio-diverse habitats in the UK, with large nature and wildlife sanctuaries. The combination of band, location and people conspires to create a strong sense of place: powerful and complex emotions are at work here.

Christopher Somerville, the writer - who is here this weekend - argues that Wilko Johnson's early Dr Feelgood songs, written for Brilleaux's voice, helped create the myth of Canvey as 'a sort of fantasy island'. It was a fantasy that all of us on the walk were keen to share. Somerville's unimprovable prose sums up our feelings well:

"Where was Dr Feelgoods' Oil City? I looked ahead and saw the burning flare stacks and mad scientist's geometry set of Shell Haven oil refinery across the creek. Further round the island a giant black jetty, remnant of a never-built refinery on Canvey itself, rose out of the fields and hurdled the mud flats of Hole Haven to curve into the River Thames. 'I've been searching, all thru' the city,' growled Brilleaux on Dr Feelgood's debut album, 'see you in the morning, down by the jetty.' Here it was, as skeletal and ominous as I'd always imagined."

Yes, but would Brilleaux like it?

Like Canvey Island, one suspects that Lee Brilleaux was not easily typecast. The onstage persona - one of controlled menace, stained suits and heavy drinking - was not the man. Brilleaux is consistently described as someone of intelligence, manners and firm principles - someone who was intense, loyal to his friends and incredibly moral. A man who 'lived life by the rules' and 'God help anyone who didn't'.

Off-stage, far from being some sort of wild man, Brilleaux was by all accounts a quiet, book-loving, crossword-completing, former trainee solicitor. In his later years, he was something of a dandy, prone to wearing cravats and expensive 'foot furniture'. He also appreciated good food and wine - as a keen home cook and an enthusiastic gourmand - and would go out of his way to find a Michelin-starred restaurant when on tour in Europe. But one thing is not in doubt: whether on or off stage, his drinking was epic.

Brilleaux inspired a huge amount of admiration and loyalty from fans and friends alike. Even fans who met him just the once sing his praises to me: a real gentleman, who always took the time to shake your hand, to speak to you in the bar, to find you a signed photograph from the murky depths of the Feelgood van and to reply to fan letters. The Governor.

Not for nothing is his authorised biography titled: 'Lee Brilleaux: Rock and Roll Gentleman'.

All who knew him agree. Brilleaux was a man who knew his own mind, who lived life by his own rules and as a result, provided a touchstone for those of us with less conviction and certainty. Tony Moon writes about the impact of Brilleaux on he and his mates, as young Feelgood fans in the 70s:

"The image that Lee evoked as a frontman became, for us, a barometer against which anything and everything could be measured and tested. For example, if we were watching something on the telly, our immediate retort would be, 'Yes, but would Lee Brilleaux like it?' For example, would Lee Brilleaux like gatefold double album sleeves? Low-tar tipped cigarettes? That style of shirt? The answer always seemed to be a very positive and life-affirming, 'NO HE FUCKIN' WOULDN'T.'"

A long time to die
By February 1993, Brilleaux had become too ill to tour. His lymphoma was terminal but, according to Chris Fenwick, such was the strength of his spirit that 'he took a long time to die'. After twenty hard-working years, playing hundreds of gigs a year, Dr Feelgood effectively disbanded while Brilleaux faced his illness.

Meanwhile, Chris Fenwick's brother had been buying up various parcels of land on Canvey Island that together became the site of the Oysterfleet Hotel. While this was going on, the original Oysterfleet - 'a shitty old pub', acquired as part of the project, says Fenwick - was converted into the Dr Feelgood Music Bar, run by Feelgood road manager and friend Dean Kennedy. Something to do while the band was off the road, says Fenwick.

In January 1994, Lee Brilleaux asked Chris Fenwick to get the band together for one last gig - his first for twelve months. For obvious reasons, this was organised at speed and took place over two nights (January 24th and 25th) at the Dr Feelgood Music Bar. Two singers - Barrie Masters and Bill Hurley – were on standby in case Lee was too weak to continue.

Neither was needed. Despite his weakened state, Brilleaux rose to the occasion admirably.

The resulting live album - Down at the Doctors - is testament to the spirit and strength of the man. It's just a really good album and the strong voice you hear seems unrelated to the obviously sick man shown on the front cover, who was apparently thin, frail and perched on a bar stool throughout, holding a walking cane.

Less than three months later, on April 7th, 1994, Lee Brilleaux passed away at his home, The Proceeds, in nearby Leigh-on Sea. He was 41 - ridiculously young, one now realises.

The first Memorial Concert

The month after Brilleaux's death, a group of his friends gathered at the Dr Feelgood Music Bar, soon to be demolished. It was agreed that a gig in honour of Lee would take place there, to raise money for SCENT - the Southend Community Extended Nursing Team - which had provided round-the-clock care at home for Lee. The event was called the Lee Brilleaux Birthday Memorial Concert and took place on his birthday: Tuesday May 10th, 1994.

There were two shows: from 1.00 to 6.00pm and from 7.00pm to midnight. The event was more jam session than concert, involving members of Eddie and the Hot Rods, The Hamsters, The Inmates, Nine below Zero, Larry Wallis and many others.

Members of Dr Feelgood past and present who played that night included Wilko Johnson, Sparko, Big Figure, Gypie Mayo, Johny Guitar, Steve Walwyn and Dave Bronze. Ace guitarist Walwyn, who is still in Dr Feelgood, claims to be the only musician to have performed at every Memorial Concert - a record of which he is justifiably proud.

This unusual - and as far as I know, unprecedented - bond between past and present band members was to become a feature of every Memorial Concert. At that first memorial concert, the three surviving founder-members of Dr Feelgood - Wilko Johnson, Sparko and The Big Figure -

played together for the first time in 15 years. There must have been a big, empty space at the front of the stage.

Twenty years of Memorial Concerts

In all, 21 Memorial Concerts have taken place, from 1994 to 2014. After that first concert at the Dr Feelgood Music Bar in 1994, they were held at a number of locations in the area: the Maritime Rooms at the Cliffs Pavilion, Southend in 1995 and 1997; and in 1996, the Grand Hotel, Leigh-On-Sea (Lee's local and the location of his interview shown in the film Oil City Confidential); settling on the upstairs function suite of the Oysterfleet Hotel from 1998 onwards.

The essence of the Memorial Concert was that it was a local event, organised and attended by people who knew Lee. Everyone - from the bands to the people on the door - gave their services for free. As well as Feelgood band members past and present, local bands Eddie and the Hot Rods and the Kursaal Flyers have been regular supporters, as have many other artists and bands, including Nine Below Zero.

All 15 'official' Feelgood members and ex-members (to qualify as 'official', they must have played 100 gigs or more with the band) have always had an open invitation to attend. All have done so, often playing in ad hoc groupings, using names like 'Gypie Mayo and the Monumentals'. Says Fenwick – 'It's a kind of a lucky dip. You don't know who you're going to see.'

Such was Brilleaux's stature that many other artists were keen to be involved in the concerts - rumour has it that Elvis Costello and Nick Lowe were among this number. However, it was decided to resist growth and to keep the event small and local - adding to the appeal and authenticity of the event. With Dr Feelgood, as with Canvey Island, what you see is what you get. You are part of the event, not a consumer of it.

For a detailed record of every Memorial Concert from 1994-2006, visit the original Dr Feelgood website, drfeelgood.de, lovingly curated by Gabi Schwanke. From Hanover, Gabi has been 'addicted' to Dr Feelgood since the early 80s and is here today.

It has been 20 eventful years and there are too many stories to recount here. The night that Chris Fenwick and Dennis the Dog swear the ghost of Lee put in an appearance, billowing curtains and all. The time Gary Loker of Eddie and the Hot Rods fell off the stage, breaking his leg in three places, to be replaced mid-song by Warren Kennedy. The evening that the PA broke down and was replaced by the bingo-callers miniature sound system, discovered under the stage.

The Last Memorial Concert

It's May 9th, the evening of the gig, and I am living the fans dream. Reclining in a leather airline seat in the Feelgood tour bus, a Mercedes, parked outside the Oysterfleet Hotel, I am ready to rock and roll. Armed with a glass of Madiran - Lee Brilleaux's favourite red wine, a case of which is always provided backstage - I am interviewing Kevin Morris, of Dr Feelgood. In the excitement, I forget what few journalistic skills I have and ask a series of banal questions, whilst imagining myself speeding across Europe on tour. Fortunately, Kevin has done this before and answers the questions I should have asked.

For the musicians, he says, the Memorial is a bit of an annual get-together, an AGM, a re-union. 'It's always been a great pleasure', says the man who has occupied the Dr Feelgood drum stool for the past 32 years, and the sense of bonhomie amongst the musicians is evident. Although unable to attend the first Memorial Concert (he and bass player Phil Mitchell were on tour with another band) Kevin has subsequently been part of the organising team with Chris Fenwick and Ann Adley.

They've done a great job for this, the final concert. 250 people are packed into the function suite of the Oysterfleet to enjoy live music from 7.45 until midnight. Tickets were sold out months ago. Tomorrow, it might be a wedding reception. Tonight, it's the last ever Lee Brilleaux Memorial Concert.

We've all piled out of the bar downstairs, not wanting to miss a thing and ready for the concert to start. First up is Shotgun. Consisting of four former Dr Feelgood band members, spanning three different eras of the band - Big Figure, Gordon Russell, Pete Gage and Sparko - this scratch outfit has had just 20 minutes rehearsal this afternoon.

Opening with I Can Tell and closing with Looking Back, Shotgun absolutely nail it. This is as close to hearing the original band as we are likely to get tonight and the crowd love it. 'Thanks to Lee for making all this possible', says Gage.

Amen to that, as the next 'act', the Reverend David Tudor, might say. The local vicar, he performs a near-miracle: he first silences, then engages and finally moves the crowd. We are putty in his hands as he recalls the words of Lee's mum, who said about Lee 'he really did have a magical life', and introduces Kelly Brilleaux, Lee's daughter. He finishes by leading us in singing two verse of Amazing Grace. Follow that!

Fortunately, next up are local boys, Eddie and the Hot Rods. Even a poor sound mix can't stop this band from being tight, loud, fast and fun. The combination of monstrous drums, pounding bass and two top-notch guitarists, fronted by a guy who is clearly loving every moment, is irresistible. That man, Barrie Masters, later tells me that when he was starting out, back in mid-70s Southend , the older Brilleaux 'was like a God to me'.

A Vicar, religious references - and I've barely started on the 'pilgrimage' analogies.

'Good evening, we're the Kursaal Flyers and we're from Sarf-end', says a heavily bearded Paul Shuttleworth. Just when we thought it couldn't get any better, it does. The band rarely performs these days, so this is a real treat, especially as this is the original line-up. While they may be a little bit rusty, a massive wave of pub-rock nostalgia washes over us, along with Vic Collins' trademark pedal steel guitar. They start with Pocket Money - 'I hate to see a nice guy without a drink' - and finish with Little Does She Know. 'We're official one-hit wonders – and here it is'.

The evening closes with Dr Feelgood – the current band. Although none are 'original' members, three of the four members were in the band with

Brilleaux over 20 years ago and even the 'new boy', singer Robert Kane, has been with the band for 15 years.

This band has every right to be called Dr Feelgood, but knows that to do this, it has to deliver every time - especially here, the home of the band. And deliver they do. Down at the Doctors leads into a set of Feelgood classics which pays tribute to all that is good about the band, without in any way being a tribute act. This is a top-class band in its own right and they sweat blood to win over the crowd. Gordon Russell comes on stage for the last two numbers and the encore - dedicated to the absent and unwell Wilko Johnson - is Route 66.

'Thangyewandgnight', as Lee Brilleaux might well have said, if he were here. And who knows, perhaps he is.

The Pilgrims

A pilgrimage needs pilgrims. The Memorial Concert has become a destination for people from all over the world: Finland, Germany, Holland, Sweden, the USA and all parts of the UK. For many, this is an AGM, a reunion - a pilgrimage perhaps. Christopher Somerville tells me that it is the 'international thing' that makes the Memorial so different and so special. Many fans have met at gigs and become friends: the Memorial is where they re-unite, providing a sense of continuity and tradition.

Many of the people I talk to speak of a sense of belonging. 'It's part of who you are', says Dave, a shadowy military figure in dark glasses ('He's MI5, he is', says Fenwick on first seeing him - and it turns out that he's not wrong). It's something you've always belonged to, they say, like a club, an occasion when you can forget your usual life and relax with fellow fans.

Agreeing with Dave, Ian from Glasgow speaks of a 'sense of purpose' that brings him back every year. Lee and the band made a huge impression in the seventies - pre-dating punk, this was music stripped back to its basics and blasted right in your face. Ian first heard Feelgood at his local youth club: 'they were the first band I heard that really excited me, that made me want to hear more.' No band since has had the same impact, I'm repeatedly told.

For many, the sense of place is important. 'It has to be Canvey' says Pecka, a consultant surgeon from Finland, and it is true that the early days of Dr Feelgood and Canvey are inter-woven. For some of the British pilgrims, Canvey is also a return to a different England, England as it used to be - the old-fashioned seaside, no ethnic diversity, no class divisions, just a 'real sense of cultural identity', as Dave puts it.

This is all a little unsettling - but rings true. I feel strangely at home here, despite being a middle-class Surrey boy these days. Canvey reminds me of 1950s Slough, where I was born, and Hayling Island, the location for childhood holidays. Slough is now the most culturally diverse town in the UK, while Canvey is the opposite.

However, the pilgrims who come to Canvey Island for this event are most certainly a diverse group, united by little other than a shared appreciation of the unique combination of place, people and music. I would like to celebrate more of them, and tell their tale, but can only mention some in passing, much as they deserve more coverage. Another time, perhaps.

First up, meet Bill Woodman and his lovely wife Susie. Bill has recently had a devastating prognosis, but is refusing to go gently into that good night. A little like Wilko Johnson (who had a terminal cancer prognosis the year before) he has continued to defy the medical profession and has been to hundreds of Feelgood gigs in recent years. Long may this continue. (Note: at the time of writing, 2021, I'm pleased to report that both Wilko and Bill are still going strong).

Feelgood has always had a very high percentage of male fans, according to Chris Fenwick - and this has always been evident at gigs over the years - but the female fans they do have are rather special. Take a bow Sally Newhouse, rock photographer, runner and all-round lifeforce extraordinaire, and Christine Kabashi, sculptor, parrot enthusiast and proud Scottish Nationalist. It has been a pleasure and privilege to meet these good people.

The Writer's Tale

Author, poet and Times journalist Christopher Somerville is an unlikely Feelgood fan. In my opinion, there is no finer writer about the UK countryside and all that it involves than this erudite and modest man who, as he admits, has somehow shoehorned Canvey Island and Dr Feelgood into his writing more than a few times.

Christopher tells me: 'I have been lucky enough to be at all of the Memorials, and at Lee's wake, too. Gypie played that old Shadows hit Wonderful Land - a real tear-starter. Dennis the Dog 'sang' House of the Rising Sun, and altogether it was a hair-up-on-back-of-neck occasion.'

In his recent book, The January Man, Somerville states that he 'can't rest satisfied if the turning circle of the year is not properly marked off with home-grown rituals - small ones, but necessary.' This enables him to mention 'fans and friends of the 'greatest local band in the world', Dr Feelgood, walking the sea walls of Canvey Island together on singer Lee Brilleaux's birthday in May.'

It is the lyrics of Wilko Johnson, original Feelgood guitarist and songwriter, as sung by Brilleaux, that first attracted Somerville.

'If a Wilko Johnson character was faced with an unfaithful girlfriend', he writes, 'he wouldn't lose his cool or burst into tears: no, he'd just rasp, 'I'm gonna get some concrete mix and fill your back door up with bricks – and you'd better be there waiting when I get my business fixed!'

He captures the essence of the Memorial Concert thus:

'I stand wedged in between Pekka and Chris, glorying in the sheer escapist pleasure of hearing those tight, razor-edged Oil City tales of drinking, cheating and losing the plot as they should be heard - live, loud, and right here in their Canvey Island birthplace.'

The Vicar's Tale

The Rev David Tudor, the Rector of Canvey Island, is a charismatic figure who has made a huge success of his ministry here.

His ever-expanding congregation fills a brand new church building, with second and third sittings at festivals like Easter. He is second on the bill at the Memorial Concert. Who would have thought that a Barbadian on this isle of whites could manage an unruly and alcohol-fuelled crowd quite so well?

A high-flier in the Church hierarchy during his early career, one suspects that he has been 'exiled' to Canvey, perhaps as some sort of punishment or test. This has been a real blessing to Canvey. As Mick, a heavy drinker testing the bar next to me, slurs, 'If he was my local Vicar, I'd definitely go to Church every week.'

The Manager's Tale

Chris Fenwick tells me that for him, this is 'one of the worst days of the year, in many ways'. Every year, he has to relive the events surrounding the death of his best friend, whilst hosting what to many is something of a jolly-up. Born Chris White (changing his name to Fenwick when he joined Equity, the actor's union), he was Lee Brilleaux's boyhood friend and has been manager of Dr Feelgood ever since. 'I never dreamed I'd be here 40 years later to tell the story', he says - but tell it he does, combining obvious emotion with the swagger and skills of the showman and professional actor that he is.

Indeed, it is Fenwick who is largely responsible for curating, controlling and disseminating the Dr Feelgood legend. However, his chosen persona of straight-talking no-nonsense band manager and hardened Essex businessman, complete with a heavy swearing habit, undoubtedly hides a much more subtle, complex and interesting individual. Brilleaux and Wilko have both been the subject of biographies – why not Chris Fenwick?

For the son of a builder who started life in a council house on Canvey Island, he has come a long way. A father who would drive the family to Morocco for holidays. A working actor and Equity card holder at age 16. Manager of Dr Feelgood in 1971, at age 18. Owner of Feelgood House at age 18. Qualified yachtsman and Thames Barge enthusiast. And more, no doubt.

Back to business: so why is this the last Memorial Concert? Fenwick isn't really saying, other than that 'it feels absolutely right'. 'We've done an honourable job for Lee' he says, and after twenty years, perhaps he feels it's best to stop while the event is still popular - as the official website stated, this was never intended to be a long-term event.

And given the situation of other band members, it could all have got rather complicated. During 2013, former member Gypie Mayo passed away and founder member Wilko Johnson came close to joining him.

The best part of the event, Fenwick tells me, is 'seeing what Lee meant to the world – the appreciation, the respect and the gratitude'. Brilleaux was always a modest man, he says, and 'if he knew about all this, he'd be chuffed to bits'.

The Daughter's Tale

Kelly Brilleaux is a lawyer in New Orleans - the home city of her mother, Lee's wife, Shirley. Kelly is a personable lady who charms everyone she meets and makes a low-key appearance on stage at the concert.

Today is her first and last memorial. Standing at the front of the crowd overlooking the Canvey marshes, she was clearly not expecting something quite so visceral, so personal, as Fenwick's detailed description of the scattering of her Father's ashes, or as moving as his stories of their childhood.

Kelly later tells me how much the whole day has meant to her. Not knowing what to expect, she is particularly impressed by the 'dedication, passion, and loyalty of the fans who participated in it from the beginning.'

This was clearly a day of mixed emotions. The walk, whilst having obvious poignancy for someone whose father died when she was nine years old, also provided a real sense of a 'shared pilgrimage', she says. As for the evening: 'the whole night truly exceeded my expectations! From start to finish, the whole room had an indescribable energy', she tells me.

Shotgun were probably the highlight, she says - 'the next best thing to getting to see my dad perform on stage' - but she enjoyed all the bands. In particular, to see the current Dr Feelgood line-up demonstrating 'the same attitude and purpose' 40 years later was something very special.

Her father, she says, 'would find it hard to believe that so many people came to pay tribute to him after all this time. I'm sure that he would be absolutely humbled and honored by the whole event.'

The donations to Havens Hospice over the years are, Kelly feels, 'the ultimate tribute to his memory.'

The Artist's Tale

'I've just killed my Mum in a car crash', says Bob Parks, in response to a question about his day, in the recently released documentary film about him, That R'n'B Feeling. And he had, falling asleep at the wheel on a trip to the local shops. Search for the trailer on Vimeo, it's well worth it.

Parks, 68, is a man for whom eccentricity has long been a way of life. A regular attendee at the Memorial Weekend, his bohemian appearance, white hair and beard, impromptu flute playing and 13-bar blues piano playing are all notable - but are not his most potent claims to fame.

A highly talented artist, with rigorous academic and intellectual underpinnings., Parks has been coming to Canvey Island since he was a child, when his Grandparents had a bungalow. He first heard R&B in an ice cream shop on Canvey in the 1950s and has been devoted to the confluence of art and R&B ever since – something he describes as 'That R&B feeling'.

As an art student, this feeling was reinforced when a lecturer played 'Let the Good Times Roll' during life classes (that's nude models to you and me). A song, ironically, that was a hit for a duo called Shirley and Lee... As a performance artist in sixties Los Angeles, he spent the best part of a year walking the streets naked and featured on the famous Gong Show in 1969. 'It all came together', he says, when he saw Dr Feelgood for the first time at the Starlight in Santa Monica in 1978.

For Parks, the Memorial is about R&B and Canvey, as well as Lee Brilleaux. The 'purity of Canvey's working-class identity' gives Dr Feelgood unique character and integrity: this could never have been a band destined for stadium tours and showbiz, he argues convincingly.

The Charity's Tale
From the first Memorial Concert onwards, all funds have been donated first to SCENT - the 'Southend Community Extended Nursing Team' which nursed Brilleaux at home – and then to its successor, local charity Havens Hospice. Over the years, more than £100,000 has been raised.

A few years ago, Havens Hospice was involved in a controversial planning application to build a £15m hospice on green belt land in Leigh-On-Sea, strongly opposed by local people. It is rumoured that the charity spent more than £100,000 on consultants, lawyers and Queen's Counsel related to this application.

To some, this makes a mockery of the money raised by the Memorial Concerts. It is unlikely that the Memorial event would have continued to support this particular charity.

The Last Memorial
Whatever your take on the demise of the Memorial, all the key people are adamant that 2014 is definitely the last. However, the memories and the music will live on. A biography of Lee Brilleaux has now been written. Founder member Wilko Johnson is higher profile than ever, having reached 'national treasure' status following his survival of a terminal cancer prognosis, and has gigs booked into 2022. The current Dr Feelgood line-up tours regularly in the UK, Europe and Scandinavia, keeping the flame burning. The back catalogue continues to sell.

I did wonder whether, a year later, Chris Fenwick would be standing alone on the Canvey Marshes, looking at Long Horse Island and thinking of Lee Brilleaux.

I later discovered that he was in Spain, in the middle of the Santiago de Compostela walk. A genuine pilgrimage, in fact.

And, in a neat twist, this is a pilgrimage route that connects with the holy city of Caravaca de la Cruz, the location for another story in this book.

Further reading and viewing
Film: Oil City Confidential
Down by the Jetty: the Dr Feelgood Story, by Tony Moon. Official band biography
www.drfeelgood.org
Lee Brilleaux, Rock and Roll Gentleman, by Zoe Howe. The authorised biography
www.christophersomerville.co.uk

ABOUT THE AUTHOR

Mark Beasley lives in the Surrey Hills, on the fringes of London, England.

For many years, he worked in advertising and marketing, where he has written or contributed to thousands of documents, proposals, presentations and reports.

During that time, no-one ever complained that a report or presentation was too short.

That's why this - his first published work of fiction – is a collection of short stories.

However, old habits die hard and it is also available in PowerPoint.

Please leave a review of this book on Amazon. It will help other potential readers - and also motivate the author to write that novel at last. If you prefer, you can contact Mark via his website.

www.markbeasley.net

Printed in Great Britain
by Amazon